THE MARQUIS DE SADE

The
Marquis de Sade

An Essay by

Simone de Beauvoir

With Selections from His Writings
Chosen by

Paul Dinnage

NEW ENGLISH LIBRARY
TIMES MIRROR

Il faut toujours en revenir a de Sade, c'est-a-dire a
l'homme naturel, pour expliquer le mal.

CHARLES BAUDELAIRE
Journaux Intimes

Simone de Beauvoir's essay was originally published in French as
'Faut-il bruler Sade?' in *Les Temps Modernes*, December, 1951
and January, 1952.
The Pensée was published in *Le Marquis de Sade* by Maurice
Heine (Paris: Gallimard, 1950). The Letter to Madame de Sade
was published in *L'Aigle, Mademoiselle . . .* , edited by Gilbert Lely
(Paris: Les Editions Georges Artigues, 1949).

© Simone de Beauvoir 1951, 1952, 1962 English translation © Paul Dinnage 1962

First published in Great Britain by John Calder (Publishers) Ltd.

*

FIRST NEL EDITION JANUARY 1972

*

NEL Books are published by
New English Library Limited from Barnard's Inn, Holborn, London E.C.1.
Made and printed in Great Britain by Hunt Barnard Printing Ltd., Aylesbury, Bucks.

450010503

CONTENTS

PART I

PART II

PART III

PART I

Must We Burn Sade?

by

SIMONE DE BEAUVOIR

MUST WE BURN SADE?

1

'Imperious, choleric, irascible, extreme in everything, with a dissolute imagination the like of which was never seen, atheistic to the point of fanaticism, there you have me in a nutshell, and kill me again or take me as I am, for I shall not change.'

They chose to kill him, first by slow degrees in the boredom of the dungeon and then by calumny and oblivion. This latter death he had himself desired. 'When the grave has been filled in, it will be sown with acorns so that eventually all trace of my tomb may disappear from the surface of the earth, just as I like to think that my memory will be effaced from the minds of men. . . . ' This was the only one of his last wishes to be respected, though most carefully so. The memory of Sade has been disfigured by preposterous legends;[1] his very name has buckled under the weight of such words as 'sadism' and 'sadistic'. His private journals have been lost, his manuscripts burned – the ten volumes of *Les Journées de Florbelle*, at the instigation of his own son – his books banned. Though in the latter part of the nineteenth century Swinburne and a few other curious spirits became interested in his case, it was not until Apollinaire that he assumed his place in French literature. However, he is still a long way from having won it officially. One may glance through heavy, detailed works on 'The Ideas of the Eighteenth Century,' or even on 'The Sensibility of the Eighteenth Century,' without once coming upon his name. It is understandable that as a reaction against this scandalous silence Sade's enthusiasts have hailed him as a prophetic genius; they claim that his work heralds Nietzsche, Stirner, Freud, and surrealism. But this cult, founded, like all cults, on a misconception by deifying the 'divine marquis' only betrays him. The critics who make of Sade neither villain nor idol, but a man and a writer can be counted upon fingers of one hand. Thanks to them, Sade has come back at last to earth, among us.

But just what is his place? Why does he merit our interest? Even his admirers will readily admit that his work is, for the most

[1] The aging Sade ordering baskets of roses to be brought to him, smelling them voluptuously and soiling them afterwards in the mud of the gutters with a sardonic laugh. Present-day journalists have taught us how this kind of anecdote is manufactured.

part, unreadable; philosophically, it escapes banality only to founder in incoherence. As to his vices, they are not startlingly original; Sade invented nothing in this domain, and one finds in psychiatric treatises a profusion of cases at least as interesting as his. The fact is that it is neither as author nor as sexual pervert that Sade compels our attention: it is by virtue of the relationship which he created between these two aspects of himself. Sade's aberrations begin to acquire value when, instead of enduring them as his fixed nature, he elaborates an immense system in order to justify them. Inversely, his books take hold of us as soon as we become aware that for all their repetitiousness their platitudes and clumsiness, he is trying to communicate an experience whose distinguishing characteristic is, nevertheless, its will to remain incommunicable. Sade tried to make of his psycho-physical destiny an ethical choice; and of this act, in which he assumed his separateness, he attempted to make an example and an appeal. It is thus that his adventure assumes a wide human significance. Can we, without renouncing our individuality, satisfy our aspirations to universality? Or is it only by the sacrifice of our individual differences that we can integrate ourselves into the community? This problem concerns us all. In Sade the differences are carried to the point of outrageousness, and the immensity of his literary effort shows how passionately he wished to be accepted by the human community. Thus, we find in his work the most extreme form of the conflict from which no individual can escape without self-deception. It is the paradox and, in a sense, the triumph of Sade that his persistent singularity helps us to define the human drama in its general aspect.

In order to understand Sade's development, in order to grasp the share of his freedom in this story, in order to assess his success and his failure, it would be useful to have precise knowledge of the facts of his situation. Unfortunately despite the zeal of his biographers, Sade's life and personality remain obscure on many points. We have no authentic portrait of him, and the contemporary descriptions which have come down to us are quite poor. The testimony at the Marseille trial shows him at thirty-two, 'a handsome figure of a man, full faced,' of medium height, dressed in a gray dress coat and deep orange silk breeches, a feather in his hat, a sword at his side, a cane in his hand. Here he is at fifty-three, according to a residence certificate dated May 7, 1793: 'Height: five feet two inches, hair almost white, round face, receding hairline, blue eyes, medium nose, round chin.' The description of March 23, 1794 is a bit different; 'Height: five feet two inches, medium nose, small mouth, round chin, grayish blond hair, high receding hairline, light blue eyes.' He seems to have lost his 'handsome figure,' since he writes a few years later, in the Bastille, 'I've taken on, for lack of exercise, such an enormous amount of fat that I can hardly move about.' It is this corpulence which first struck Charles Nodier when he met Sade in 1807 at Sainte-Pelagie. 'An immense obesity which hindered his movements so as to prevent the exercise of those remains of grace and elegance which still lingered in his general comportment. There remained, nevertheless, in his weary eyes an indefinable flash and brilliance which took fire from time to time, like a dying spark on a dead coal.' These testimonies, the only ones we possess, hardly enable us to visualize a particular face. It has been said[2] that Nodier's description recalls the aging Oscar Wilde; it suggests Montesquiou and Maurice Sachs as well, and it tempts us to imagine a bit of Charlus in Sade, but the data is very weak.

Even more regrettable is the fact that we have so little information about his childhood. If we take the account of Valcour for an autobiographical sketch, Sade came to know resentment and violence at an early age. Brought up with Louis-Joseph de Bourbon his contemporary, he seems to have defended himself against the selfish arrogance of the young prince with such displays of anger and brutality that he had to be taken away from court. Probably his stay in the gloomy château of Saumane and in the decaying abbey of Ebreuil left its mark upon his imagination, but we know nothing significant about his brief years of study, his entry into the army, or his life as an *amiable* man of fashion and debauchee. One might try to deduce his life from his work; this has been done by Klossowski, who sees in Sade's implacable hatred of his mother the key to his life and work. But he derives this hypothesis from the mother's role in Sade's writings. That is, he restricts himself to a description of Sade's imaginary world from a certain angle. He does not reveal its roots in the real world. In fact, we suspect a priori, and in accordance with certain general notions, the importance of Sade's relationship with his father and mother; the particular details are not available to us. When we meet Sade he is already mature, and we do not know how he has become what he is. Ignorance forbids us to account for his tendencies and spontaneous behavior. His emotional nature and the peculiar character of his sexuality are for us data which we can merely note. Because of this unfortunate gap, the truth about Sade will always remain closed to us; any explanation would leave a residue which only the childhood history of Sade might have clarified.

Nevertheless, the limits imposed on our understanding ought

[2] Jean Desbordes, *Le Vrai Visage du Marquis de Sade* (Paris, 1939).

not to discourage us, for Sade, as we have said, did not restrict himself to a passive submission to the consequences of his early choices. His chief interest for us lies not in his aberrations, but in the manner in which he assumed responsibility for them. He made of his sexuality an ethic; he expressed this ethic in works of literature. It is by this deliberate act that Sade attains a real originality. The reason for his tastes is obscure, but we can understand how he erected these tastes into principles.

Superficially, Sade, at twenty-three, was like all other young aristocrats of his time; he was cultured, liked the theater and the arts, and was fond of reading. He was dissipated, kept a mistress – la Beauvoisin – and frequented the brothels. He married, without enthusiasm and in conformance to parental wishes, a young girl of the petty aristocracy, Renée-Pélagie de Montreuil, who was, however, rich. That was the beginning of the disaster that was to resound – and recur – throughout his life. Married in May, Sade was arrested in October for excesses committed in a house which he had been frequenting since June. The reasons for arrest were grave enough for Sade to send letters, which went astray, to the governor of the prison, begging him to keep them secret, lest he be hopelessly ruined. This episode suggests that Sade's eroticism had already assumed a disquieting character. This hypothesis is confirmed by the fact that a year later Inspector Marais warned the procuresses to stop giving their girls to the Marquis. But the interest of all this lies not in its value as information, but in the revelation which it constituted for Sade himself. On the verge of his adult life he made the brutal discovery that there was no conciliation possible between his social existence and his private pleasures.

There was nothing of the revolutionary nor even of the rebel about young Sade. He was quite prepared to accept society as it was. At the age of twenty-three he was obedient enough to his father[3] to accept a wife whom he disliked, and he envisaged no other life than the one to which his heredity destined him. He was to become a husband, father, marquis, captain, lord of the manor, and lieutenant general. He had not the slightest wish to renounce the privileges assured by his rank and his wife's fortune. Nevertheless, these things could not satisfy him. He was offered activities, responsibilities, and honors; nothing, no simple venture interested, amused, or excited him. He wished to be not only a public figure, whose acts are ordained by convention and routine, but a live

[3] Klossowski is surprised by the fact that Sade bore his father no ill will. But Sade did not instinctively detest authority. He admits the right of the individual to exploit and to abuse his privileges. At first, Sade, who was heir to the family fortune, fought society only on the individual, emotional level, through women: his wife and mother-in-law.

human being as well. There was only one place where he could assert himself as such, and that was not the bed in which he was received only too submissively by a prudish wife, but in the brothel where he bought the right to unleash his fantasies.

And there was one dream common to most young aristocrats of the time. Scions of a declining class which had once possessed concrete power, but which no longer retained any real hold on the world, they tried to revive symbolically, in the privacy of the bedchamber the status for which they were nostalgic, that of the lone and sovereign feudal despot. The orgies of the Duke of Carolais, among others, were bloody and famous. Sade, too, thirsted for this illusion of power. 'What does one want when one is engaged in the sexual act? That everything about you give you its utter attention, think only of you, care only for you . . . every man wants to be a tyrant when he fornicates.' The intoxication of tyranny leads directly to cruelty, for the libertine, in hurting the object that serves him, 'tastes all the pleasures which a vigorous individual feels in making full use of his strength; he dominates, he is a tyrant.'

Actually, whipping a few girls (for a consideration agreed upon in advance) is rather a petty feat; that Sade sets so much store on it is enough to cast suspicion upon him. We are struck by the fact that beyond the walls of his 'little house' it did not occur to him to 'make full use of his strength.' There is no hint of ambition in him, no spirit of enterprise, no will to power, and I am quite prepared to believe that he was a coward. He does, to be sure, systematically endow his heroes with traits which society regards as flaws, but he paints Blangis with a satisfaction that justifies the assumption that this is a projection of himself, and the following words have the direct ring of a confession: 'A determined child might have frightened this colossus . . . he grew timid and cowardly, and the idea of an equally matched fight, however safe, would have sent him fleeing to the ends of the earth.' The fact that Sade was at times capable of extravagant boldness, both out of rashness and generosity, does not invalidate the hypothesis that he was afraid of people and, in a more general way, afraid of the reality of the world.

If he talked so much about his strength of soul, it was not because he really possessed it, but because he longed for it. When faced with adversity, he would whine and get upset and become completely distraught. The fear of want which haunted him constantly was a symptom of a much more generalized anxiety. He mistrusted everything and everybody because he felt himself maladjusted. He was maladjusted. His behavior was disorderly.

13

He accumulated debts; he would fly into a rage for no reason at all, would run away, or would yield at the wrong moment. He fell into every possible trap. He was uninterested in this boring and yet threatening world which had nothing valid to offer him and from which he hardly knew what to ask. He was to seek his truth elsewhere. When he writes that the passion of jealousy 'subordinates' and 'at the same time unites' all other passions, he gives us an exact description of his own experience. He subordinated his existence to his eroticism because eroticism appeared to him to be the only possible fulfillment of his existence. If he devoted himself to it with such energy, shamelessness, and persistence, he did so because he attached greater importance to the stories he wove around the act of pleasure than to the contingent happenings; he chose the imaginary.

At first Sade probably thought himself safe in the fool's paradise which seemed separated from the world of responsibility by an impenetrable wall. And perhaps, had no scandal broken out, he would have been but a common debauchee, known in special places for rather special tastes. Many libertines of the period indulged with impunity in orgies even worse. But scandal was probably inevitable in Sade's case. There are certain 'sexual perverts' to whom the myth of Dr Jekyll and Mr. Hyde is perfectly applicable. They hope, at first, to be able to gratify their 'vices' without compromising their public characters. If they are imaginative enough to visualize themselves, little by little, in a dizziness of pride and shame, they give themselves away – like Charlus, despite his ruses, and even because of them. To what extent was Sade being provocative in his imprudence? There is no way of knowing. He probably wished to emphasize the radical separation between his family life and his private pleasures, and probably, too, the only way he could find satisfaction in this clandestine triumph lay in pushing it to the point where it burst forth into the open. His surprise is that of the child who keeps striking at a vase until it finally breaks. He was playing with fire and still thought himself master, but society was lying in wait. Society wants undisputed possession. It claims each individual unreservedly. It quickly seized upon Sade's secret and classified it as crime.

Sade reacted at first with prayer, humility, and shame. He begged to be allowed to see his wife, accusing himself of having grievously offended her. He begged to confess and open his heart to her. This was not mere hypocrisy. A horrible change had taken place overnight; natural, innocent practices, which had been hitherto merely sources of pleasure, had become punishable acts. The young charmer had changed into a black sheep. He had probably been familiar since childhood – perhaps through his relations with his mother – with the bitter pangs of remorse, but the scandal of 1763 revived them dramatically. Sade had a foreboding that he would henceforth and for the rest of his life be a culprit. For he valued his diversions too highly to think, even for a moment, of giving them up. Instead, he rid himself of shame through defiance. It is significant that his first deliberately scandalous act took place immediately after his imprisonment. La Beauvoisin accompanied him to the château of La Coste and, taking the name of Madame Sade, danced and played before the Provençal nobility, while the Abbé de Sade was forced to stand dumbly by. Society denied Sade illicit freedom; it wanted to socialize eroticism. Inversely, the Marquis' social life was to take place henceforth on an erotic level. Since one cannot, with any peace of mind, separate good from evil and devote one's self to each in turn, one has to assert evil in the face of good, and even as a function of good.

Sade tells us repeatedly that his ultimate attitude has its roots in resentment. 'Certain souls seem hard because they are capable of strong feelings, and they are sometimes very distant; their apparent unconcern and cruelty are but ways, known only to themselves, of feeling more strongly than others.'[4] And Dolmancé[5] attributes his vice to the wickedness of men. 'It was their ingratitude which dried up my heart, their treachery which destroyed in me those baleful virtues for which, like you, I may have been born.' The fiendish morality which he later established in theoretical form was first a matter of actual experience.

It was through Renée-Pélagie that Sade came to know all the insipidity and boredom of virtue. He lumped them together in the disgust which only a creature of flesh and blood can arouse. But he learned also from Renée, to his delight, that Good, in concrete, fleshly, individual form, can be vanquished in single combat. His wife was not his enemy, but like all the wife-characters she inspired, a choice victim, a willing accomplice. The relationship between Blamont and his wife is probably a fairly precise reflection of Sade's with the Marquise. Blamont takes pleasure in caressing his wife at the very moment that he is hatching the blackest plots against her. To inflict enjoyment – Sade understood this 150 years before the psychoanalysts, and his works abound in victims submitted to pleasure before being tortured – can be a tyrannical violence; and the torturer disguised as lover delights to see the credulous lover, swooning with voluptuousness and gratitude,

---

[4] *Aline et Valcour.*
[5] *La Philosophie dans le Boudoir.*

mistake cruelty for tenderness. The joining of such subtle pleasures with the performance of social obligation is doubtless what led Sade to have three children by his wife.

And he had the further satisfaction of seeing virtue become the ally of vice, and its handmaiden. Madame de Sade concealed her husband's delinquencies for years; she bravely engineered his escape from Miolans, fostered the intrigue between her sister and the Marquis, and later, lent her support to the orgies at the château of La Coste. She went even so far as to inculpate herself when, in order to discredit the accusations of Nanon, she hid some silverware in her bags. Sade never displayed the least gratitude. In fact, the notion of gratitude is one at which he keeps blasting away most furiously. But he very obviously felt for her the ambiguous friendship of the despot for what is unconditionally his. Thanks to her, he was able not only to reconcile his role of husband, father, and gentleman with his pleasures, but he established the dazzling superiority of vice over goodness, devotion, fidelity, and decency, and flouted society prodigiously by submitting the institution of marriage and all the conjugal virtues to the caprices of his imagination and senses.

If Renée-Pélagie was Sade's most triumphant success, Madame de Montreuil embodies his failure. She represents the abstract and universal justice which inevitably confronts the individual. It was against her that he most eagerly entreated his wife's support. If he could win his case in the eyes of virtue, the law would lose much of its power, for its most formidable arms were neither prison nor the scaffold, but the venom with which it could infect vulnerable hearts. Renée became perturbed under the influence of her mother. The young canoness grew fearful. A hostile society invaded Sade's household and dampened his pleasures, and he himself yielded to its power. Defamed and dishonored, he began to doubt himself. And that was Madame de Montreuil's supreme crime against him. A guilty man is, first of all, a man accused; it was she who made a criminal of Sade. That is why he never left off ridiculing her, defaming her, and torturing her throughout his writings; he was killing off his own faults in her. There is a possible basis for Klossowski's theory that Sade hated his own mother; the singular character of his sexuality suggests this. But this hatred would never have been inveterate had not Renée's mother made motherhood hateful to him. Indeed, she played such an important and frightful role that it may well be that she was the sole object of his attack. It is certainly she, in any case, whom he savagely submits to the jeers of her own daughter in the last pages of *La Philosophie dans le Boudoir.*

16

If Sade was finally beaten by his mother-in-law and by the law, he was accomplice to this defeat. Whatever the role of chance and of his own imprudence in the scandal of 1763, there is no doubt that he afterwards sought a heightening of his pleasures in danger. We may therefore say that he desired the very persecutions which he suffered with indignation. Choosing Easter Sunday to decoy the beggar, Rose Keller, into his house at Arcueil meant playing with fire. Beaten, terrorized, inadequately guarded, she ran off, raising a scandal for which Sade paid with two short terms in prison.

During the following three years of exile which, except for a few periods of service, he spent on his property in Provence, he seemed sobered. He played the husband and lord of the manor most conscientiously. He had two children by his wife, received the homage of the community of Saumane, attended to his park, and read and produced plays in his theater, including one of his own. But he was ill-rewarded for this edifying behavior. In 1771, he was imprisoned for debt. Once he was released, his virtuous zeal cooled off. He seduced his young sister-in-law, of whom he seemed, for a while, genuinely fond. She was a canoness, a virgin, and his wife's sister, all of which lent a certain zest to the adventure. Nevertheless, he went to seek still other distractions in Marseille, and in 1772 the 'affair of the aphrodisiac candies' took on unexpected and terrifying proportions. While in flight to Italy with his sister-in-law he and Latour, his valet, were sentenced to death in absentia, and both of them were burned in effigy on the town square of Aix. The canoness took refuge in a French convent, where she spent the rest of her life, and he hid away in Savoy. He was caught and locked up in the château of Miolans, but his wife helped him escape. However, he was henceforth a hunted man. Whether roaming through Italy or shut up in his castle, he knew that he would never be allowed a normal life.

Occasionally, he took his lordly role seriously. A troupe of actors was staying on his property to give *The Cuckold, Whipped and Happy*. Sade, irritated perhaps by the title, ordered that the posters be defaced by the town clerk, as being 'disgraceful and a challenge to the freedom of the Church.' He expelled from his property a certain Saint-Denis, against whom he had certain grievances, saying, 'I have every right to expel all loafers and vagrants from my property.' But these acts of authority were not enough to amuse him. He tried to realize the dream which was to haunt his books. In the solitude of the château of La Costa, he set up for himself a harem submissive to his whims. With the aid of the Marquise, he gathered together several handsome valets, a secretary who was illiterate but attractive, a luscious cook, a chamber-maid, and two young girls provided by bawds. But La Coste was not the inaccessible fortress of *Les 120 Journées de Sodome;* it was surrounded by society. The maids escaped, the chambermaid left to give birth to a child whose paternity she attributed to Sade, the cook's father came to shoot Sade, and the handsome secretary was sent for by his parents. Only Renée-Pélagie conformed to the character assigned to her by her husband; all the others claimed the right to live their own lives, and Sade was once again made to understand that he could not turn the real world of hard fact into a theater.

This world was not content to thwart his dreams; it repudiated him. Sade fled to Italy, but Madame de Montreuil, who had not forgiven him for having seduced her younger daughter, lay in wait for him. When he got back to France, he ventured into Paris, and she took advantage of the occasion to have him locked up on the 13th of February, 1777, in the château of Vincennes. He was brought to trial and sent back to Aix and took refuge at La Coste, where, under the resigned eye of his wife, he embarked on an idyl with his housekeeper, Mademoiselle Rousset. But by the 7th of November, he was back again at Vincennes, 'locked up behind nineteen iron doors, like a wild beast.'

And now begins another story. For eleven years – first at Vin-cennes and then in the Bastille – a man lay dying in captivity, but a writer was being born. The man was quickly broken. Reduced to impotence, not knowing how long his imprisonment would last, his mind wandered in delirious speculation. With minute cal-culations, though without any facts to work on, he tried to figure out how long his sentence would last. He recovered possession of his intellectual powers fairly quickly, as can be seen from his correspondence with Madame de Sade and Mademoiselle Rousset. But the flesh surrendered, and he sought compensation for his sexual starvation in the pleasures of the table. His valet, Carteron, tells us that 'he smoked like a chimney' and 'ate enough for four men' while in prison. Extreme in everything, as he himself declares, he became wolfish. He had his wife send him huge hampers of food, and he grew increasingly fat. In the midst of complaints, accusations, pleas, supplications, he still amused himself a bit by torturing the Marquise; he claimed to be jealous, accused her of plotting against him, and when she came to visit him, found fault with her clothes and ordered her to dress with extreme austerity. But these diversions were few and pallid. From 1782 on, he deman-ded of literature alone what life would no longer grant him: excitement, challenge, sincerity, and all the delights of the imagination. And even then, he was 'extreme'; he wrote as he ate, in a frenzy. After *Dialogue entre un prêtre et un moribond* came *Les 120 Journées de Sodome, La Novelle Justine, Aline et Valcour.* According to the catalogue of 1788, he had by then writen 35 acts for the theater, half a dozen tales, almost all of *Le Portefeuille d'un homme de lettres*, and the list is probably still incomplete.

When Sade was freed, on Good Friday of 1790, he could hope and did hope that a new period lay open before him. His wife asked for a separation. His sons (one was preparing to emigrate and the other was a Knight of Malta) were strangers to him; so was his 'good, husky farm wench' of a daughter. Free of his family, he whom the old society had called an outcast was now going to try to adapt himself to the one which had just restored to him his dignity as a citizen. His plays were performed in public; *Oxtiern* was even a great success; he enrolled in the *Section des Piques* and was appointed president; he enthusiastically wrote speeches and drew up petitions. But idyll with the Revolution did not last long. Sade was fifty years, old, had a questionable past and an aristocratic disposition, which his hatred of the aristocracy had not subdued, and he was once again at odds with himself. He was a republican and, in theory, even called for complete socialism and the abolition of property, but insisted on keeping his castle and properties. The world to which he tried to adapt himself was again an all too real world whose brutal resistance wounded him. And it was a world governed by those universal laws which he regarded as abstract, false, and unjust. When society justified murder in their name, Sade withrew in horror.

Anyone who is surprised at Sade's discrediting himself by his humaneness instead of seeking a governor's post in the provinces, a post that would have enabled him to torture and kill to his heart's content does not really understand Sade. Does anyone suppose that he 'liked blood' the way one likes the mountains or the sea? 'Shedding blood' was an act whose meaning could, under certain conditions, excite him, but what he demanded, essentially, of cruelty was that it reveal to him particular individuals and his own existence as, on the one hand, consciousness and freedom and, on the other, as flesh. He refused to judge, condemn, and witness anonymous death from afar. He had hated nothing so much in the old society as the claim to judge and punish, to which he himself had fallen victim; he could not excuse the Terror. When murder becomes constitutional, it becomes merely the hateful expression of abstract principles, something without content, inhuman. And this is why Sade as Grand Juror almost always dismissed the charges against the accused. Holding their fate in his hands, he refused to harm the family of Madame de Montreuil in the name of the law. He was even led to resign from his office of president of the *Section des Piques*. He wrote to Gaufridy, 'I considered myself obliged to leave the chair to the vice-president; they wanted me to put a horrible, an inhuman act to a vote. I never would.' In December, 1793, he was imprisoned on charges of 'moderantism.' Released 375 days later, he wrote with disgust, 'My government imprisonment, with the guillotine before my eyes, did me a hundred times more harm than all the imaginary Bastilles.' It is by such whoesale slaughters that the body politic shows only too obviously that it considers men as a mere collection of objects, whereas Sade demanded a universe peopled with individual beings. The 'evil' which he had made his refuge vanished when crime was justified by virtue. The Terror, which was being carried out with a clear conscience, constituted the most radical negation of Sade's demoniacal world.

'The excesses of the Terror,' wrote Saint-Just, 'have dulled the taste for crime.' Sade's sexuality was not stilled by age and fatigue alone; the guillotine killed the morbid poetry of eroticism. In order to derive pleasure from the humiliation and exaltation of the flesh, one must ascribe value to the flesh. It has no sense, no worth, once one casually begins to treat man as a thing. Sade was still able to revive his past experience and his old universe in his books, but he no longer believed in them with his blood and nerves. There is nothing physical in his attachment to the woman he calls 'The Sensitive Lady.' He derived his only erotic pleasures from the contemplation of the obscene paintings, inspired by Justine, with which he decorated a secret chamber. He still had his memories, but he had lost his drive, and the simple business of living was too much for him. Liberated from the social and familial framework which he nevertheless needed, he dragged on through poverty and illness. He quickly ran through the money realized from the unprofitable sale of La Coste. He took refuge with a farmer, and then in a garret, with a son of 'The Sensitive Lady,' while earning forty sous a day working in the theatricals at Versailles.

The decree of June 28, 1799, which forbade the striking of his name from the list of aristocratic emigrés on which it had been placed, made him cry out in despair, 'Death and affliction; these are the rewards of my constant attachment to the Republic.' He received, however, a certificate of residence and citizenship; and in December, 1799, he played the part of Fabrice in *Oxtiern*. But by the beginning of 1800, he was in the hospital of Versailles, 'dying of hunger and cold,' and threatened with imprisonment for debt. He was so unhappy in the hostile world of so-called 'free' men that one wonders whether he had not chosen to be led back to the solitude and security of prison. We may say, at least, that the imprudence of circulating *Justine* and the folly of publishing *Zoloé*, in which he attacks Joséphine, Tallien, Madame Tallien, Barras, and Bonaparte, imply that he was not too repelled by the idea of another confinement. Conscious or not, his wish was granted; he was locked up in Sainte-Pélagie on April 5, 1801, and it was there and later at Charenton – where he was followed by Madame Quesnet, who, by pretending to be his daughter, obtained a room near his own – that he lived out the rest of his life.

Of course, Sade protested and struggled as soon as he was shut up, and he continued to do so for years. But at least he was able again to devote himself in peace to the passion which had replaced sensual pleasure, his writing. He wrote on and on. Most of his papers had been lost when he left the Bastille, and he thought that the manuscript of *Les 120 Journées de Sodome* – a fifteen-yard roll which he had carefully hidden and which was saved without his knowing it – had been destroyed. After *La Philosophie dans le Boudoir*, written in 1795, he composed a new opus, a modified and completely developed version of *Justine*, followed by *Juliette*, of which he disclaimed the authorship and which appeared in 1797. He had *Les Crimes de l'Amour* publicly printed. At Sainte-Pélagie, he became absorbed in an immense, ten-volume work, *Les Journées de Florbelle*. The two volumes of *La Marquis de Ganges* must also be attributed to him, though the work appeared without his name.

Probably because the meaning of his life lay henceforth in his work as a writer, Sade now hoped only for peace in his daily life. He took walks with 'The Sensitive Lady' in the garden of the retreat, wrote comedies for the patients, and had them performed. He agreed to compose a *divertissement* on the occasion of a visit by the Archbishop of Paris. On Easter Sunday, he distributed the holy bread and took up the collection in the parish church. His will proves that he had renounced none of his beliefs, but he was tired of fighting. 'He was polite to the point of obsequiousness,' says Nodier, 'gracious to the point of unctiousness ... and he spoke respectfully of everything the world respects.' According to Ange Pitou, the ideas of old age and of death horrified him. 'This man turned pale at the idea of death, and would faint at the sight of his white hair.' He expired in peace, however, carried off by 'a pulmonary congestion in the form of asthma' on December 2, 1814.

The sailent feature of his tormented life was that the painful experience of living never revealed to him any solidarity between

21

other men and himself. The last scions of a decadent aristocracy had no common purpose to unite them. In the solitude to which his birth condemned him, Sade carried erotic play to such extremes that his peers turned against him. When a new world opened to him, it was too late; he was weighed down with too heavy a past. At odds with himself, suspect to others, this aristocrat, haunted dreams of despotism, could not sincerely ally himself with the rising bourgeoisie. And though he was roused to indignation by its oppression of the people, the people were nevertheless foreign to him. He belonged to none of the classes whose mutual antagonisms were apparent to him. He had no fellow but himself. Perhaps, had his emotional make-up been different, he might have resisted this fate, but he seems always to have been violently egocentric. His indifference to external events, his obsessive concern with money, the finical care with which he worked out his debauches, as well as the delirous speculations at Vincennes and the schizophrenic character of his dreams, reveal a radically introverted character. Though this passionate self-absorption defined his limits, it also gave his life an exemplary character, so that we examine it today.

2

Sade made of his eroticism the meaning and expression of his whole existence. Thus, it is no idle curiosity that leads us to define its nature. To say with Maurice Heine that he tried everything and and liked everything is to beg the question. The term 'algolagnia' hardly helps us to understand Sade. He obviously had very marked sexual idiosyncrasies, but they are not easy to define. His accomplices and victims kept quiet. Two flagrant scandals merely pushed aside, for a moment, the curtain behind which debauch usually hides. His journals and memoirs have been lost, his letters were cautious, and in his books, he invents more than he reveals about himself. 'I have imagined everything conceivable in this sort of thing,' he writes, 'but I have certainly not done, and certainly never will, all that I've imagined.' His work has not unreasonably been compared to the *Psychopathie Sexualis* of Krafft-Ebing, to whom no one would dream of attributing all the perversions he catalogued.

Thus, Sade established systematically, according to the prescriptions of a kind of synthetic art, a repertory of man's sexual possibilities. He certainly never experienced nor even dreamed them all up himself. Not only does he tell tall stories, but most of the time, he tells them badly. His tales resemble the engravings that illustrate the 1797 edition of *Justine* and *Juliette*. The characters' anatomy and positions are drawn with a minute realism, but the awkward and monotonous expressionlessness of their faces makes their horrible orgies seem utterly unreal. It is not easy to derive a genuine testimony from all the cold-blooded orgies that Sade concocted. Nevertheless, there are some situations in his novels which he treats with special indulgence. He shows special, sympathy with some of his heroes, for example, Noirceuil, Blangis and Gernande, and particularly Dolmancé, to whom he attributes many of his own tastes and ideas. Sometimes, too, in a letter, an incident, or a turn of dialogue, we are struck unexpectedly by a vivid phrase which we feel is not the mere echo of a foreign voice. It is precisely such scenes, heroes, and texts as these that we must examine closely.

In the popular mind, sadism means cruelty. The first thing that strikes us in Sade's work is actually that which tradition associates with his name: beatings, bloodshed, torture, and murder. The Rose Keller incident shows him beating his victim with a cat-o'-nine-tails and a knotted cord and, probably,[6] slashing her with a knife and pouring wax on the wounds. In Marseille, he took from his pockets a parchment 'cat' covered with bent nails and asked for switches of heather. In all his behaviour towards his wife, he displayed obvious mental cruelty. Moreover, he has expressed himself over and over on the pleasure to be derived from making people suffer. But he hardly enlightens us when he merely repeats the classical doctrine of animal spirits. 'It is simply a matter of jangling all our nerves with the most violent possible shock. Now, since there can be no doubt that pain affects us more strongly than pleasure, when this sensation is produced in others, our very being will vibrate more vigorously with the resulting shocks.' Sade does not eliminate the mystery of the conscious pleasure which follows from this violent vibration. Fortunately, he suggests more honest explanations elsewhere.

The fact is that the original intuition which lies at the basis of Sade's entire sexuality, and hence his ethic, is the fundamental identity of coition and cruelty. 'Would the paroxysm of pleasure be a kind of madness if the mother of the human race [Nature] had not intended that anger and the sexual act express themselves in the same way? What able-bodied man . . . does not wish . . . to bedevil his ecstasy?' Sade's description of the Duke of Blangis in the throes of orgasm is certainly to be interpreted as a transposition in epic terms of Sade's own practices. 'Horrible shrieks and dreadful oaths escaped his heaving breast. Flames seemed to dart from

---

[6] Sade's confessions do not corroborate Rose Keller's testimony on this point.

his eyes. He frothed at the mouth, he whinnied . . . ' and he even strangled his partner. According to Rose Keller's testimony, Sade himself 'began to shriek very loud and fearfully' before cutting the cords which immobilized his victim. The 'Vanilla and Manilla' letter proves that he experienced orgasm as if it were an epileptic seizure, something aggressive and murderous, like a fit of rage.

How are we to explain this peculiar violence? Some readers have wondered whether Sade was not, in fact, sexually deficient. Many of his heroes, among them his great favorite, Gernande, are inadequately equipped, and have great difficulty in erection and ejaculation. Sade must certainly have been familiar with such fears, but this semi-impotence seems rather to have been the result of execessive indulgence, as in the case of many of his debauchees, several of whom are very well endowed. Sade makes frequent allusions to his own vigorous temperament. It is, on the contrary, a combination of passionate sexual appetites with a basic emotional 'apartness' which seems to me to be the key to his eroticism.

From adolescence to prison, Sade had certainly known the insistent, if not obsessive, pangs of desire. There is, on the other hand, an experience which he seems never to have known: that of emotional intoxication. Never in his stories does sensual pleasure appear as self-forgetfulness, swooning, or abandon. Compare, for example, Rousseau's outpourings with the frenzied blasphemies of a Noirceuil or a Dolmancé, or the flutters of the Mother Superior in Diderot's *La Religieuse* with the brutal pleasures of Sade's tribades. The male aggression of the Sadist hero is never softened by the usual transformation of the body into flesh. He never, for an instant, loses himself in his animal nature; he remains so lucid, so cerebral, that philosophic discourse, far from dampening his ardor, acts as an aphrodisiac. We see how desire and pleasure explode in furious attacks upon this cold, tense body, proof against all enchantment. They do not constitute a living experience within the framework of the subject's psychophysiological unity. Instead, they blast him, like some kind of bodily accident.

As a result of this immoderateness, the sexual act creates the illusion of sovereign pleasure which gives it its incomparable value in Sade's eyes; for all his sadism strove to compensate for the absence of one necessary element which he lacked. The state of emotional intoxication allows one to grasp existence in one's self and in the other, as both subjectivity and passivity. The two partners merge in this ambiguous unity; each one is freed of his own presence and achieves immediate communication with the other. The curse which weighed upon Sade – and which only his childhood could explain – was this 'autism' which prevented him from ever forgetting himself or being genuinely aware of the reality of the other person. Had he been cold by nature, no problem would ever have arisen; but his instincts drove him toward outside objects with which he was incapable of uniting, so that he was forced to invent singular methods for taking them by force. Later when his desires were exhausted, he continued to live in that erotic universe of which, out of sensuality, boredom, defiance, and resentment, he had constructed the only world which counted for him; and the aim of his strategies was to induce erection and orgasm. But even when these were easy for him, Sade needed deviations to give to his sexuality a meaning which lurked in it without ever managing to achieve fulfillment an escape from consciousness in his flesh, an understanding of the other person as consciousness through the flesh.

Normally, it is as a result of the vertigo of the other made flesh that one is spellbound within his own flesh. If the subject remains confined within the solitude of his consciousness, he escapes this agitation and can rejoin the other only by conscious performance. A cold, cerebral lover watches eagerly the enjoyment of his mistress and needs to affirm his responsibility for it because he has no other way of attaining his own fleshy state. This behavior, which compensates for separateness by deliberate tyranny, may be properly called 'sadistic.' Sade knew, as we have seen, that the infliction of pleasure may be an aggressive act, and his tyranny sometimes took on this character, but it did not satisfy him. To begin with, he shrinks from the kind of equality which is created by mutual pleasure. 'If the objects who serve us feel ecstasy, they are then much more often concerned with themselves than with us, and our own enjoyment is consequently impaired. The idea of seeing another person experience the same pleasure reduces one to a kind of equality which spoils the unutterable charms that come from despotism.' And he declares, more categorically, 'Any enjoyment is weakened when shared.'

And besides, pleasant sensations are too mild; it is when the flesh is torn and bleeding that it is revealed most dramatically as flesh. 'No kind of sensation is keener and more active than that of pain; its impressions are unmistakable.' But in order for me to become flesh and blood through the pains I have inflicted, I must recognize my own state in the passivity of the other. Therefore, the person must have freedom and consciousness. The libertine 'would really deserve pity if he acted upon an inert, unfeeling object.' That is why the contortions and moans of the victim are necessary to the torturer's happiness, which explains why Verneuil made his wife wear a kind of headgear that amplified her screams. In his revolt, the tortured object asserts himself as my fellow creature, and through his intervention I achieve the synthesis of spirit and flesh which was first denied me.

If the aim is both to escape from one's self and to discover the reality of other existences, there is yet another way open; to have one's flesh mortified by others. Sade is quite aware of this. When he used the 'cat' and the switch in Marseille, it was not only to whip others with, but also to be whipped himself. This was probably one of his most common practices, and all his heroes happily submit to flagellation. 'No one doubts these days that flagellation is extremely effective in restoring the vigor destroyed by the excesses of pleasure.' There was another way of giving concrete form to his passivity. In Marseille, Sade was sodomized by his valet, Latour, who seems to have been accustomed to render him this sort of service. His heroes imitate him sedulously, and he declared aloud in no uncertain terms that the greatest pleasure is derived from a combination of active and passive sodomy. There is no perversion of which he speaks so often and with so much satisfaction, and even impassioned vehemence.

Two questions immediately arise for those given to labeling individuals. Was Sade a sodomite? Was he basically masochistic? As to sodomy, his physical appearance, the role played by his valets, the presence at La Coste of the handome, illiterate secretary, the enormous importance which Sade accords to this 'fantasy' in his writings, and the passion with which he advocates it, all confirm the fact that it was one of the essential elements of his sexual character. Certainly, women played a great role in his life, as they do in his work. He knew many, had kept La Beauvoisin and other, less important mistresses, had seduced his sister-in-law, had gathered young women and little girls together at the château of La Coste, had flirted with Mademoiselle Rousset, and finished his days at the side of Madame Quesnet, to say nothing of the bonds, imposed by society but reworked in his own fashion, which united him with Madame de Sade. But what were his relations with her? It is significant that in the only two testimonies on his sexual activity, there is no evidence that Sade 'knew' his partners in a normal way. In Rose Keller's case, he satisfied himself by whipping her without touching her. He asked the Marseille prostitute to let herself be 'known from behind' by his servant or, if she preferred, by himself. When she refused, he contented himself with fondling her while he was being 'known' by Latour.

His heroes amuse themselves by deflowering little girls. This

26

bloody and sacrilegious violence tickled Sade's fancy. But even when they are initiating virgins, they often treat them as boys rather than make them bleed. More than one of Sade's characters feels a deep disgust for women's 'fronts'. Others are more eclectic in taste, but their preferences are clear. Sade never sang that part of the female body so joyously celebrated in *The Arabian Nights*. He has only contempt for the poor 'unmanly creatures' who possess their wives in conventional fashion. If he had children by Madame de Sade, we have seen under what circumstances; and in view of the strange group orgies at La Coste, what proof is there that it was really he who was responsible for Nanon's pregnancy?

We must not, of course, attribute to Sade the opinions held by the confirmed homosexuals of his novels ,but the argument put into the mouth of the bishop in *Les 120 Journées de Sodome* is close enough to his heart to be considered as a confession. He says, concerning pleasure, 'A boy is better than a girl. Consider him from the viewpoint of the evil which is almost always pleasure's real attraction. The crime committed with a creature completely like yourself seems greater than that with one who is not, and thus the pleasure is doubled.' It was easy enough for Sade to write to Madame de Sade that his sole wrong had been 'to love women too much'; this was a purely official and hypocritical letter. And it is through a mythical dialectic that he gives them the most triumphant roles in his novels. Their wickedness makes a striking contrast with the traditional gentleness of their sex. When they overcome their natural abjection by committing crime, they demonstrate much more brilliantly than any man that no situation can dampen the ardor of a bold spirit. But if, in imagination, they become first-rate martinets, it is because they are, in reality, born victims.

The contempt and disgust which Sade really felt for these servile, tearful, mystified, and passive creatures runs all through his work. Was it his mother whom he loathed in them? We may also wonder whether Sade did not hate women because he saw in them his double rather than his complement and because there was nothing he could get from them. His great female villains have more warmth and life than his heroes, not only for aesthetic reasons but because they were closer to him. I do not recognize him at all, as some readers claim to, in the bleating Justine, but there is certainly something of him in Juliette, who proudly and contentedly submits to the same treatment as her sister. Sade felt himself to be feminine, and he resented the fact that women were not the males he really desired. He endows Durand, the greatest and most extravagant of them all, with a huge clitoris which enables her to

27

behave sexually like a man.

It is impossible to tell to what extent women were anything but surrogates and toys for Sade. It may be said, however, that his sexual character was essentially anal. This is confirmed by Sade's attachment to money. Trouble involving embezzlement of inheritances played an enormous role in his life. Theft appears in his work as a sexual act, and the mere suggestion of it is enough to cause orgasm. And though we may refuse to accept the Freudian interpretation of greed, there is the indisputable fact, which Sade openly acknowledged, of his coprophilia. In Marseille, he gave a prostitute some sugar almonds, telling her that 'they would make her break wind,' and he looked disappointed when nothing happened. We are also struck by the fact that the two *fantaisies* which he tries to explain most fully are cruelty and coprophagy. To what extent did he practice them? It is a far cry from the practices begun in Marseille to the excremental orgies of *Les 120 Journées de Sodome*, but the care with which he describes the latter practices, and particularly the preparations, proves that they were not merely cold and schematic inventions, but emotional fantasies.

On the other hand, Sade's extraordinary gluttony in prison cannot be explained by idleness alone. Eating can be a substitute for erotic activity only if there is still some infantile equivalence between gastrointestinal and sexual functions. This certainly persisted in Sade. He sees a close bond between the food orgy and the erotic orgy. 'There is no passion more closely involved with lechery than drunkenness and gluttony,' he points out. And this combination reaches a climax in anthropophagous fantasies. To drink blood, to swallow sperm and excrement, and to eat children mean appeasing desire through destruction of its object. Pleasure requires neither exchange, giving, reciprocity, nor gratuitous generosity. Its tyranny is that of avarice, which chooses to destroy what it cannot assimilate.

Sade's coprophilia has still another meaning. 'If it is the dirty element that gives pleasure in the act of lust, then the dirtier it is, the more pleasurable it is bound to be.' Among the most obvious sexual attractions, Sade includes old age, ugliness, and bad odors. His linking of eroticism with *vileness* is as original as his linking it with cruelty, and can be explained in like manner. Beauty is too simple. We grasp it by an intellectual evaluation which does not free consciousness from its solitude or the body from its indifference, whereas vileness is debasing. The man who has relations with filth, like the man who wounds or is wounded, fulfills himself as flesh. It is in its misery and humiliation that the flesh becomes a gulf in which consciousness is swallowed up and where separate

28

individuals are united. Only by being beaten, penetrated, and befouled could Sade succeed in destroying its obsessive presence.

He was not, however, masochistic in the ordinary sense of the word. He sneers bitterly at men who become slaves to women. 'I leave them to the base pleasure of wearing the chains with which Nature has given them the right to burden others. Let such animals vegetate in the baseness of their abjection.' The world of the masochist is a magical one, and that is why he is almost always a fetishist. Objects, such as shoes, furs, and whips, are charged with emanations which have the power to change him into a thing, and and that is precisely what he wants, to remove himself by becoming an inert object. Sade's world is essentially rational and practical. The objects, whether material or human, which serve his pleasure are tools which have no mystery, and he clearly sees humiliation as a haughty ruse. Saint-Fond, for example, says, 'The humiliation of certain acts of debauchery serves as a pretext for pride.' And Sade elsewhere says of the libertine that 'the degradation which characterizes the state into which you plunge him by punishing him pleases, amuses, and delights him. Deep down he enjoys having gone so far as to deserve being treated in such a way.'

Nevertheless, these two attitudes are intimately related. If the masochist wants to lose himself, he does so in order to be entranced by the object with which he hopes to merge, and this effort leads him back to his subjectivity. In demanding that his partner mistreat him, he tyrannizes over him; his humiliating exhibitions and tortures he undergoes humiliate and torture the other as well. And, vice versa, by befouling and hurting the other, the torturer befouls and hurts himself. He participates in the passivity which he discloses, and in wanting to apprehend himself as the cause of the torment he inflicts, it is as an instrument and therefore as an object that he perceives himself. We are thus justified in classing behavior of this kind under the name of sadomasochism. However, we must be careful, for despite the generality of the term, the concrete forms of this behavior may be quite varied. Sade was not Sacher-Masoch. What was peculiar in his case was the tension of a will bent on fulfilling the flesh without losing itself in it. In Marseille, he had himself whipped, but every couple of minutes he would dash to the mantelpiece and, with a knife, would inscribe on the chimney flue the number of lashes he had just received. His humiliation would immediately be transformed into swagger. While being sodomized, he would whip a prostitute. It was a favorite fantasy of his to be penetrated and beaten while he himself was penetrating and beating a submissive victim.

I have already said that to regard Sade's peculiarities as simple facts is to misunderstand their meaning and implication. They are always charged with an ethical significance. With the scandal of 1763, Sade's eroticism ceased to be merely an individual attitude: it was also a challenge to society. In a letter to his wife, Sade explains how he has erected his tastes into principles. 'I carry these principles and tastes to the point of fanaticism,' he writes, 'and the fanaticism is the work of my tyrants and their persecutions.' The supreme intention that quickens all sexual activity is the will to criminality. Whether through cruelty or befoulment, the aim is to attain evil. Sade immediately experienced coitus as cruelty, laceration, and transgression; and out of resentment he obstinately justified its morbidity. Since society united with Nature in regarding his pleasures as criminal, he made crime itself a pleasure. 'Crime is the soul of lust. What would pleasure be if it were not accompanied by crime? It is not the object of debauchery that excites us, but rather the idea of evil.' In the pleasure of torturing and mocking such a woman, he writes, 'there is the kind of pleasure which comes from sacrilege or the profanation of the objects offered us for worship.' It was not by chance that he chose Easter as the day to whip Rose Keller, and it was at the moment that he sardonically suggested that he confess her that his sexual excitement reached its climax. No aphrodisiac is so potent as defiance of the Good. 'Our desires for great crimes are always more violent than our desires for small ones.' Did Sade do evil in order to feel guilty, or did he escape guilt by assuming it? To reduce him to one or another of these attitudes is to deform him. He never remains at rest in a state either of self-satisfied abjection or of flighty impudence, but keeps oscillating back and forth dramatically between arrogance and a guilty conscience.

Thus, we can perceive the significance of Sade's cruelty and masochism. This man, who combined a violent temperament – though quickly exhausted, it would seem – with an emotional 'apartness' almost pathological in character, sought a substitute for anxiety in the infliction of suffering or pain. The meaning of his cruelty is very complex. In the first place, it seems to be the extreme and immediate fulfillment of the instinct of coitus, its total assumption. It asserts the radical separation of the other object from the sovereign subject. It aims at the jealous destruction of what cannot be greedily assimilated. But above all, rather than crowning the orgasm impulsively, it tends to induce it by premeditation. It enabled him to apprehend through the other person the consciousness-flesh unity and to project it into himself. And, lastly, it freely justified the criminal character which nature and society had assigned to eroticism. Moreover, by being sodomized, beaten, and befouled, Sade also gained insight into himself as passive flesh. He slaked his thirst for self-punishment and accepted the guilt to which he had been doomed. And this enabled him to revert immediately from humility to pride through the medium of defiance. In the completely sadistic scene, the individual gives vent to his nature, fully aware that it is evil and aggressively assuming it as such. He merges vengeance and transgression and transforms the latter into glory.

There is one act which stands as the most extreme conclusion of both cruelty and masochism, for the subject asserts himself in it, in a very special way, as tyrant and criminal; I am speaking of murder. It has often been maintained that murder was the supreme end of sexuality in Sade. To my mind, this view is based on a misunderstanding. Certainly the vigor with which Sade denied in his letters that he had ever been a murderer was a matter of self-defense, but I think that he was sincerely repelled by the idea. He does, of course, overload his stories with monstrous slaughters. But he does so because there is no crime whose abstract significance is so glaringly obvious as murder. It represents the exacerbated demand for unrestrained and fearless freedom. And besides, by indefinitely prolonging the death throes of his victim, the author can perpetuate on paper the exceptional moment in which a lucid mind inhabits a body which is being degraded into matter. He still breathes a living past into the unconscious remains. But what would the tyrant actually do with this *inert object*, a corpse?

There is, no doubt, something vertiginous in the transition from life to death; and the sadist, fascinated by the conflicts between consciousness and the flesh, readily pictures himself as the agent of so radical a transformation. But though he may occasionally carry out this singular experiment, it cannot possibly afford him the supreme satisfaction. The freedom that one hoped to tyrannize to the point of annihilation has, in being destroyed, slipped away from the world in which tyranny had a hold on it. If Sade's heroes commit endless massacres, it is because none of them gives full satisfaction. They bring no concrete solution to the problems which torment the debauchee, because pleasure is not his sole end. No one would seek sensation so passionately and recklessly, even if it had the violence of an epileptic seizure. The ultimate trauma must, rather, guarantee by its obviousness the success of an undertaking, whose stake exceeds it infinitely. But often, however, it stops it without concluding it, and though it may be prolonged by murder, the murder merely confirms its failure.

Blangis strangles his partners with the very fury of orgasm, and there is despair in the rage wherein desire is extinguished

31

without satisfaction. His premeditated pleasures are less wild and more complex. An episode from *Juliete*, among others, is significant. Excited by the young woman's conversation, Noirceuil who 'cared little for solitary pleasures,' that is, those in which one indulges with a single partner, immediately calls in his friends. 'There are too few of us. . . . No, leave me. . . My passions, concentrated upon this single point, are like the beams of the sun focused by a lens. They immediately burn any object brought into focus.' It is not out of any abstract scruples that he forbids himself such excesses, but rather because after the brutal orgasm he would find himself frustrated again. Our instincts indicate to us ends which are unattainable if we merely act upon our immediate impulses. We must master them, reflect upon them, and use our wits in trying to find ways of satisfying them. The presence of other consciousnesses than our own is what helps us most to get the necessary perspective on them.

Sade's sexuality is not a biological matter. It is a social fact. The orgies in which he indulged were almost always collective affairs. In Marseille, he asked for two prostitutes and was accompanied by his valet. At La Coste, he set up a harem for himself. The libertines in his novels form actual communities. The first advantage was the number of combinations for their debauches, but there were deeper reasons for the socialization of eroticism. In Marseille, Sade called his valet 'Monsieur le Marquis' and wanted to see him 'know' a prostitute under his name rather than 'know' her himself. The enactment of the erotic scene interested him more than the actual experience. The fantasies in *Les 120 Journées de Sodome* are narrated before being carried out. By means of this duplication the act becomes a spectacle which one observes from a distance at the same time that one is performing it. It thus retains the meaning that would otherwise be obscured by solitary animal excitement. For if the debauchee coincided exactly with his movements and the victim with his emotions, freedom and consciousness would be lost in the rapture of the flesh. The flesh would be merely brute suffering, and the rapture merely convulsive pleasure. Thanks, however, to the assembled witnesses, a presence is maintained about them which helps the subject himself remain present. It is through these performances that he hopes to reach out to himself; and in order to see himself, he must be seen. Sade, while tyrannizing, was an object for those who watched him.

Vice versa, by witnessing on the flesh to which he had done violence the violence which he himself had borne, he repossessed himself as subject within his own passivity. The merging of the for-oneself and the for-the-other is thus achieved. Accomplices are particularly required in order to give sexuality a demoniacal dimension. Thanks to them, the act, whether committed or suffered, takes on definite form instead of being diluted into contingent moments. By becoming real, any crime proves to be possible and ordinary. One gets to be so intimately familiar with it that one had difficulty in regarding it as blameworthy. In order to amaze or frighten oneself, one must observe oneself from a distance, through foreign eyes.

However precious this recourse to others may be, it is not yet enough to remove the contradictions implied in the sadistic effort. If one fails, in the course of an actual experience, to grasp the ambiguous unity of existence, one will never succeed in reconstructing it intellectually. A spectacle, by definition, can never coincide with either the inwardness of consciousness or the opacity of the flesh. Still less can it reconcile them. Once they have been dissociated, these two moments of the human reality are in opposition to each other; and as soon as we pursue one of them, the other disappears. If the subject inflicts excessively violent pain upon himself, his mind becomes unhinged: he abdicates; he loses his sovereignty. Excessive vileness entails disgust, which interferes with pleasure. In practice, it is difficult to indulge in cruelty, except within very modest limits; and in theory, it implies a contradiction which is expressed in the following two passages: 'The most divine charms are as nothing when submission and obedience do not come forth to offer them,' and 'One must do violence to the object of one's desire; when it surrenders, the pleasure is greater.' But where is one to find free slaves? One has to be satisfied with compromises. With paid and abjectly consenting prostitutes, Sade went somewhat beyond the limits that had been agreed upon. He allowed himself some violence against a wife who maintained a certain human dignity in her docility.

But the ideal erotic act was never to be realized. This is the deeper meaning of the words Sade puts into the mouth of Jerome: 'What we are doing here is only the image of what we would like to do.' It was not merely that really heinous crimes were forbidden in practice, but that even those which one could summon up in the midst of the wildest ravings would disappoint their author: 'To attack the sun, to deprive the universe of it or to use it to set the world ablaze – these would be crimes indeed!' But if this dream seemed satisfying, it was because the criminal projected into it his own destruction along with that of the universe. Had he survived, he would have been frustrated once again. Sadistic crime can never be adequate to its animating purpose. The victim is never more than a symbol; the subject possesses himself only as an imago, and their relationship is merely the parody of the drama which would really set them at grips in their incommunicable intimacy. That is why the bishop in *Les 120 Journées de Sodome* 'never committed a crime without immediately conceiving a second.'

The moment of plotting the act is an exceptional moment for the libertine because he can then be unaware of the inevitable fact, that reality will give him the lie. And if narration plays a primary role in Sadistic orgies and easily awakens senses upon which flesh-and-blood objects cease to act, the reason is that these objects can be wholly attained only in their absence. Actually there is only one way of finding satisfaction in the phantoms created by debauchery, and that is to accede to their very unreality. In choosing eroticism, Sade chose the make-believe. It was only in the imaginary that Sade could live with any certitude and without risk of disappointment. He repeated the idea throughout his work. 'The pleasure of the senses is always regulated in accordance with the imagination.' 'Man can aspire to felicity only by serving all the whims of his imagination.' It was by means of his imagination that he escaped from space, time, prison, the police, the void of absence, opaque presences, the conflicts of existence, death, life, and all contradictions. It was not murder that fulfilled Sade's erotic nature; it was literature.

3

It might seem, at first glance, that by writing Sade was merely reacting as many other prisoners do in the same situation. The idea was not completely new to him. One of the plays presented at La Coste in 1772 was probably written by him; and his strong-box, forced open by order of Madame de Montreuil, contained certain 'leaflets,' probably notes on sex, in his own hand. Nevertheless, when he was imprisoned at Vincennes, he waited four years before undertaking a real work. In another cell of the same fortress, Mirabeau, who was also groaning that he was 'being buried alive in a tomb,' tried to divert himself by doing translations writing an essay on the *lettres de cachet*, and carrying on a pornographic correspondence. He was trying to kill time, to distract his weary body, and to undermine a hostile society. Sade was driven by similar motives; he set to work; and more than once, while composing his novels, he *had to whip himself up*. He also wanted to revenge himself on his torturers. He writes to his wife in a joyous rage, 'I'll wager you imagined you were working wonders in reducing me to agonizing abstinence from the sins of the flesh. Well! you were quite mistaken . . . you've made me create phantoms which I must bring to life.'

Although his decision may have been prompted by his confinement, nevertheless it had much deeper roots. Sade had always spun stories for himself around his debauches; and the reality which served as a frame of reference for his fantasies may have given them a certain density, yet it also cramped them by its resistance. The opacity of things blurs their significance, which is the very quality which words preserve. Even a child is aware that crude drawings are more obscene than the organs and gestures which they represent, because the intention to defile is asserted in all its purity. Blasphemy is the easiest and surest of sacrilegious acts. Sade's heroes talked on and on indefatigably; and in the Rose Keller affair he indulged in endless speechifying. Writing is far more able than the spoken word to endow images with the solidity of a monument, and it resists all argument. Thanks to the written word, virtue maintains her dreary prestige even at the very moment when she is denounced as hypocrisy and stupidity. Crime remains criminal in its grandeur. Freedom may still throb in a dying body.

Literature enabled Sade to unleash and fix his dreams and also to transcend the contradictions implied by any demonic system. Better still, it is itself a demonic act since it exhibits criminal visions in an aggressive way. That is what gives it its incomparable value. Anyone misunderstands Sade who finds it paradoxical that a 'solitary' should have engaged in such a passionate effort to communicate. He had nothing of the misanthrope who prefers the company of animals and virgin forests to his own kind. Cut off from others, he was haunted by their inaccessible presence.

Did he wish only to shock? In 1795 he wrote, 'I shall present you with great truths; people will listen and give thought to them. Though not all may find favor, some at least will remain. I shall have contributed in some way to the progress of enlightenment, and I shall be content.'[7] And in *La Nouvelle Justine*, 'To falsify such basic truths, regardless of their consequences, reveals a fundamental lack of concern for human beings.' After presiding over the *Section des Piques* and drawing up speeches and petitions in society's name, he must have liked, in his more optimistic moments, to think of himself as a spokesman for humanity. Of this experience he retained not the evil aspects, but those which were genuinely rewarding. These dreams quickly faded, but it would

[7] *La Philosophie dans le Boudoir.*

35

be too simple to consign Sade to satanism. His sincerity was inextricably bound up with dishonesty. He delighted in the shocking effects of truth; but if he set himself the duty of shocking, it was because in this way truth might be made manifest. While arrogantly admitting his errors, he declared himself in the right. He wished to transmit a message to the very public he was deliberately outraging. His writings reflect the ambivalence of his relation to the given world and to people.

What might surprise us even more is the mode of expression he chose. We might expect a man who had so jealously cultivated his singularity to try to translate his experience into a singular form, as, for example, Lautréamont did. But the eighteenth century offered Sade few lyrical possibilities; he hated the mawkish sensibility which the time confused with poetry – the time was not yet ripe for a *poete maudit*. And Sade was in no way disposed to great literary audacity. A real creator should, at least on a certain level and at a given moment, free himself of the yoke of the *given* and emerge beyond other men into complete solitude. But there was in Sade an inner weakness which was inadequately masked by his arrogance. Society was lodged in his heart in the guise of guilt. He had neither the means nor the time to reinvent man, the world, and himself. He was in too much of a hurry, in a hurry to defend himself. I have already said that he sought in writing to gain a clear conscience; and in order to do this, he had to compel people to absolve him, even to approve him. Instead of affirming himself, Sade argued; and in order to make himself understood, he borrowed the literary forms and the tried and tested doctrines of contemporary society. To the product of a rational age, no arm seemed surer to him than reason. He who wrote, 'All universal moral principles are idle fancies' submitted docilely to general aesthetic conventions and contemporary claims for the universality of logic. This explains both his art and his thought. Though he justified himself, he was always trying to excuse himself. His work is an ambiguous effort to push crime to the extreme while wiping away his guilt.

It is both natural and striking that Sade's favorite form was parody. He did not try to set up a new universe. He contented himself with ridiculing, by the manner in which he imitated it, the one imposed upon him. He pretended to believe in the vain fancies that inhabited it; innocence, kindness, devotion, generosity and chastity. When he unctuously depicted virtue in *Aline et Valcour*, in *Justine*, or in *Les Crimes de l'Amour*, he was not being merely prudent. The 'veils' in which he swathed Justine were more than a literary device. In order to derive amusement from

36

harassing virtue, one must credit it with a certain reality. Defending his tales against the charge of immorality, Sade hypocritically wrote, 'Who can flatter himself that he has put virtue in a favorable light if the features of the vice surrounding it are not strongly emphasized?' But he meant the very opposite: how is vice to be made thrilling if the reader is not first taken in by the illusion of good? Fooling people is even more delicious than shocking them. And Sade, in spinning his sugary, roundabout phrases, tasted the keen pleasures of mystification. Unfortunately, he generally amuses himself more than he does us. His style has often the same coldness and the same insipidity as the edifying tales he transposed, and the episodes unfold in accordance with equally dreary conventions.

Nevertheless, it was through parody that Sade obtained his most brilliant artistic successes. As Maurice Heine points out, Sade was the precursor of the novel of horror, but he was too deeply rationalistic to lose himself in fantasy. When he abandons himself to the extravagances of his imagination, one does not know which to admire the most, his epic vehemence or his irony. The wonder is that the irony is subtle enough to redeem his ravings. It lends, on the contrary, a dry, poetic quality which saves them from incredibility. This somber humor which can, at times, turn on itself, is more than a mere technique. With his shame and pride, his truth and crime, Sade was the very spirit of contentiousness. It is when he plays the buffoon that he is really most serious, and when he is most outrageously dishonest, that he is most sincere. His extravagance often masks ingenuous truths, while he launches the most flagrant enormities in the form of sober and deliberate arguments; he uses all kinds of tricks to avoid being pinned down; and that is how he attains his end, which is to disturb us. His very form tends to disconcert us. He speaks in a monotonous embarrassed tone, and we begin to be bored, when all at once the dull grayness is lit up with the glaring brilliance of some bitter, sardonic truth. It is then that Sade's style, in its gaiety, its violence, and its arrogant rawness, proves to be that of a great writer.

Nevertheless, no one would think of ranking *Justine* with *Manon Lescaut* or *Les Liaisons Dangereuses*. It was, paradoxically, the very necessity of Sade's work which imposed upon it its aesthetic limits. He did not have the perspective essential to an artist. He lacked the detachment necessary to confront reality and recreate it. He did not confront himself; he contented himself with projecting his fantasies. His accounts have the unreality, the false precision, and the monotony of schizophrenic reveries. He relates them for his own pleasure, and he is unconcerned about imposing

37

them upon the reader. We do not feel in them the stubborn resistance of the real world or the more poignant resistance that Sade encountered in the depths of his own heart. Caves, underground passageways, mysterious castles, all the props of the Gothic novel take on a particular meaning in his work. They symbolize the isolation of the image. Perception echoes data's totality and, consequently, the obstacles which the data contain. The image is perfectly submissive and pliant. We find in it only what we put into it. The image is the enchanted domain from which no power whatever can expel the solitary despot. It is the image that Sade was imitating, even while claiming to give it literary opacity. Thus, he disregarded the spatial and temporal coordinates within which all real events are situated. The places he evokes are not of this world, the events which occur in them are tableaux rather than adventures, and time has no hold on Sade's universe. There is no future either for or in his work.

Not only do the orgies, to which he invites us, take place in no particular time or locality, but – what is more serious – no living people are brought into play. The victims are frozen in their tearful abjection, and the torturers in their frenzies. Instead of giving them lifelike density, Sade merely daydreams about them. Remorse and disgust are unknown to them; at most they have occasional feelings of satiety. They kill with indifference; they are abstract incarnations of evil. But unless eroticism has some social, familial, or human basis, it ceases to be in any way extraordinary. It is no longer a conflict, a revelation, or an exceptional experience. It no longer reveals any dramatic relationship between individuals but reverts to biological crudity. How is one to feel the opposition of others' freedoms or the spirit's descent into the flesh, if all we see is a display of voluptuous or tortured flesh? Horror itself peters out in these excesses at which no consciousness is actually present. If a story like Poe's 'The Pit and the Pendulum' is so full of anguish, it is because we grasp the situation from within the subject; we see Sade's heroes only from without. They are as artificial and move in a world as arbitrary as that of Florian's shepherds. That is why these perverse bucolics have the austerity of a nudist colony.

The debauches which Sade describes in such great detail systematically exhaust the anatomical possibilities of the human body but they do not reveal uncommon emotional complexes. Nevertheless, though he failed to endow them with aesthetic truth, Sade adumbrated forms of sexual behavior unknown until then, particularly those which unite mother-hatred, frigidity, intellectuality, 'passive sodomy,' and cruelty. No one has emphaisized with more vigor and link between the imagination and what we call vice; and he gives us from time to time, insights of surprising depth into the relation of sexuality to existence.

Are we, then, to admire him as a real innovator in psychology? It is difficult to decide. Forerunners are always credited with either too much or too little. How is one to measure the value of a truth which, to use Hegel's term, has not *become*? An idea derives its value from the experience it sums up and the methods it initiates. But we hardly know what credit to give a new and attractive formulation if it is not confirmed by further developments. We are tempted either to magnify it with all the significance that it acquires later on or else to minimize its scope. Hence, in the case of Sade, the impartial reader hesitates. Often, as we turn a page, we come upon an unexpected phrase which seems to open up new paths, only to find that the thinking stops short. Instead of a vivid and individual voice, all one hears is the droning drivel of Holbach and La Mettrie.

It is remarkable, for example, that in 1795[8] Sade wrote, 'Sexual pleasure is, I agree, a passion to which all others are subordinate but in which they all unite.' Not only does Sade, in the first part of this text, anticipate what has been called the 'pansexuality' of Freud, but he makes of eroticism the mainspring of human behavior. In addition, he asserts, in the second part, that sexuality is charged with a significance that goes beyond it. Libido is everywhere, and it is always far more than itself. Sade certainly anticipated this great truth. He knew that the 'perversions that are vulgarly regarded as moral monstrosities or physiological defects actually envelop what would now be called an intentionality. He writes to his wife that all 'fancy . . . derives from a principle of delicacy,' and in *Aline et Valcour* he declares that 'refinements come only from delicacy; one may, therefore, have a great deal of delicacy, though one may be moved by things which seem to exclude it.' He understood, too, that our tastes are motivated not by the intrinsic qualities of the object but by the latter's relationship with the subject. In a passage in *La Nouvelle Justine* he tries to explain coprophilia. His reply is faltering, but clumsily using the notion of imagination, he points out that the truth of a thing lies not in what it is but in the meaning it has taken on for us in the course of our individual experience. Intuitions such as these allow us to hail Sade as a precursor of psychoanalysis.

Unfortunately, he reduces their value when he insists upon harping, like Holbach, on the principles of psychophysiological parallelism. 'With the perfecting of the science of anatomy, we

8 *Ibid.*

shall easily be able to show the relationship between man's constitution and the tastes which have affected him.' The contradiction is glaring in the striking passage in *Les 120 Journées de Sodome* where he considers the sexual attraction of ugliness. 'It has moreover, been proved that horror, nastiness, and the frightful are what give pleasure when one fornicates. Beauty is a simple thing; ugliness is the exceptional thing. And fiery imaginations, no doubt, always prefer the extraordinary thing to the simple thing.' One might wish that Sade had defined this link between horror and desire which he indicates only confusedly; but he stops abruptly with a conclusion that cancels the question that has been posed: 'All these things depend upon our structures and organs and on the manner in which they affect one another, and we are no more able to change our tastes for these things than to vary the shapes of our bodies.'

At first glance, it seems paradoxical that this man who was so self-centered should have given such prominence to theories which deny any significance to individual peculiarities. He asks that we make a great effort to understand the human heart better. He tries to explore its strangest aspects. He cries out, 'What an enigma is man!' He boasts, 'You know that no one analyzes things as I do,' and yet he follows La Mettrie in lumping man together with the machine and the plant and simply does away with psychology. But this antinomy, disconcerting though it may be, is easily explained. It is probably not so easy to be a monster as some people seem to think. Sade, though fascinated by his own personal mystery, was also frightened by it. Instead of expressing himself, he wanted to defend himself. The words he puts into Blamont's mouth[9] are a confession: 'I have supported my deviations with reasons; I did not stop at mere doubt; I have vanquished I have uprooted, I have destroyed everything in my heart that might have interfered with my pleasures.' The first of these tasks of liberation was, as he repeated countless times, to triumph over remorse. And as for repudiating all feelings of guilt, what doctrine could be surer than that which undermines the very idea of responsibility? But it would be a big mistake to try to confine him to such a notion: if he seeks support in determinism, he does so, like many others, in order to lay claim to freedom.

From a literary point of view, the commonplace-ridden speeches with which he intersperses his debauches finally rob them of all life and all verisimilitude. Here, too, it is not so much the reader to whom Sade is talking, but himself. His wearisome repetitions are tantamount to a purification rite whose repetition is as natural

[9] *Aline et Valcour.*

to him as regular confession is to a good Catholic. Sade does not give us the work of a free man. He makes us participate in his efforts of liberation. But it is precisely for this reason that he holds our attention. His endeavor is more genuine that the instruments it employs. Had Sade been satisfied with the determinism he professed, he should have repudiated all his moral anxieties. But these asserted themselves with a clarity that no logic could obscure. Over and above the facile excuses which he sets forth so tediously, he persists in questioning himself, in attacking. It is owing to this headstrong sincerity that, though not a consummate artist or a coherent philosopher, he deserves to be hailed as a great moralist.

4

'Extreme in everything,' Sade could not adapt himself to the deist compromises of his time. It was with a declaration of atheism, *Dialogue entre un prêtre et un moribond*, that in 1782 he launched his work. The existence of God had been denied more than once since the appearance in 1729 of *Le Testament du curé de Meslier*. Rousseau had dared to present a sympathetic atheist, Monsieur de Wolmar, in *La Nouvelle Héloïse*. In spite of this, the Abbé Mélégan had been thrown into prison in 1754 for having written *Zoroastre;* and La Mettrie was obliged to take refuge at the court of Frederick II. The atheism vehemently espoused by Sylvain Maréchal and popularized by Holbach, in *Le Système de la Nature* of 1770 and by the satires collected under the title *Recueil philosophique*, was nonetheless a dangerous doctrine in an age which placed the scaffold itself under the aegis of the Supreme Being. Sade, in parading his atheism, was deliberately committing a provocative act. But it was also an act of sincerity. I feel that Klossowski, despite the interest of his study, is misinterpreting Sade in taking his passionate rejection of God for an avowal of need. The sophism which maintains that to attack God is to affirm Him finds a great deal of support these days, but this notion is actually the invention of those to whom atheism is a challenge. Sade expressed himself clearly on the matter when he wrote, 'The idea of God is the sole wrong for which I cannot forgive mankind.'

And if this is the first mystification he attacks, it is because he proceeds, like a good Cartesian, from the simple to the complex, from the gross lie to the more misleading error. He knows that in order to free the individual from the idols to which society has bound him, one must begin by ensuring his independence in the face of heaven. If man had not been terrorized by the great bug-bear to which he stupidly pays worship, he would not so easily have surrendered his freedom and truth. In choosing God, he denied himself, and that was his unpardonable offence. Actually, he is responsible to no transcendent judge; there is no heavenly court of appeal.

Sade was not unaware of the extent to which the belief in hell and eternity might inflame cruelty. Saint-Fond toys with such hopes so as to extract pleasure from the limitless suffering of the damned. He diverts himself by imagining a diabolical demiurge who would embody the diffuse evil of Nature. But not for one instant did Sade consider these hypotheses as anything more than intellectual pastimes. He is not to be recognized in the char-acters who express them, and he refutes them through his mouth-pieces. In evoking absolute crime, his aim is to ravage Nature and not to wound God. His harangues against religion are open to reproach because of the tedious monotony with which they repeat timeworn commonplaces; but Sade gives them still another personal turn when, anticipating Nietzsche, he denounces in Christianity a religion of victims which ought, in his view, to be replaced by an ideology of force. His honesty, in any case, is unquestionable. Sade's nature was thoroughly irreligious. There is no trace of metaphysical anxiety in him; he is too concerned with justifying his existence to speculate on its meaning and purpose. His convictions on the subject were wholehearted. If he served at mass and flattered a bishop, it was because, old and broken, he had chosen hypocrisy. But his testament is unequivocal. He feared death for the same reason that he feared senility. The fear of the beyond never appears in his work. Sade wished to deal only with men, and everything that was not human was foreign to him.

And yet he was alone among men. The eighteenth century, in so far as it tried to abolish God's reign upon earth, substituted another idol in its place. Atheists and deists united in the worship of the new incarnation of the Supreme Good: Nature. They had no intention of forgoing the conveniences of a categorical, universal morality. Transcendental values had broken down; pleasure was acknowledged as the measure of good; and through this hedonism, self-love was reinstated. For example, Madame du Chatelet wrote, 'We must begin by saying to ourselves that we have nothing else to do in this world but seek pleasant sensations and feelings.' But these timid egotists postulated a natural order which assured the harmonious agreement of individual interests with the general interest. A reasonable organization, obtained by

42

pact or contract, would suffice to ensure the prosperity of society for the benefit of all and each. Sade's tragic life gave the lie to this optimistic religion.

The eighteenth century often painted love in somber, solemn, and even tragic tones; and Richardson, Prévost, Duclos, and Crébillon, whom Sade quotes with respect, and, above all, Laclos, whom Sade claimed not to know, created more or less satanic heroes. But their wickedness always has its source, not in spontaneity, but in a perversion of their minds or wills. Quite the contrary, genuine eroticism, because of its instinctive character, is reinstated. Natural, healthy, and useful to the species, sexual desire merges, according to Diderot, with the very movement of life, and the passions it brings are likewise good and fruitful. If the characters in *La Religieuse* take pleasure in 'sadistic' viciousness, it is because instead of satisfying their appetites they repress them. Rousseau, whose sexual experience was complex and largely unhappy, also expresses this in edifying terms: 'Sweet pleasures, pure, vivid, painless, and unalloyed.' And also: 'Love, as I see it, as I have felt it, grows ardent before the illusory image of the beloved's perfection, and this very illusion leads it to enthusiasm for virtue. For this idea always enters into that of the perfect woman.'[10] Even in Restif de la Bretonne, though pleasure may have a stormy character, it is nonetheless rapture, languor, and tenderness. Sade was the only one to reveal selfishness, tyranny, and crime in sexuality. This would suffice to give him a unique place in the history of the sensibility of his century, but from this insight he derived even more remarkable ethical consequences.

There was nothing new in the idea that Nature is evil. Hobbes, with whom Sade was familiar and whom he quotes freely, had declared that man is a wolf to man and that the state of Nature is one of war. A long line of English moralists and satirists had followed in his steps, among them Swift, whom Sade used and even copied. In France, Vauvenargues continued the puritan and Jansenist development of the Christian tradition which identifies the flesh with original sin. Bayle and, more brilliantly, Buffon established the fact that Nature is not wholly good; and though the myth of the Noble Savage had been current since the sixteenth century, particularly in Diderot and the Encyclopedists, Emeric de Crucé had already attacked it at the beginning of the eighteenth century. Sade had no trouble finding any number of arguments to support the thesis which was implied in his erotic experience and

---

[10] Cf. Sade: 'It is horror, vileness, the frightful, which give pleasure when one fornicates. Where are they more likely to be found than in a corrupt object? Many people prefer for their pleasure an old, ugly, even a stinking woman to a fresh and pretty girl.'

which was ironically confirmed by society's imprisoning him for having followed his instincts. But what distinguishes him from his predecessors is the fact that they, after exposing the evil of Nature, set up, in opposition to it, a morality which derived from God and society; whereas Sade, though rejecting the first part of the generally accepted credo; 'Nature is Good; let us follow her,' paradoxically retained the second. Nature's example has an imperative value, even though her law be one of hate and destruction. We must now examine more closely the ruse whereby he turned the new cult against its devotees.

Sade conceived the relation of man to Nature in various ways. These variations seem to me not so much the movements of a dialectic as the expressions of the hesitation of a thinking that at times restrains its boldness and at others breaks completely loose. When Sade is merely trying to find hasty justifications, he adopts a mechanistic view of the world. La Mettrie affirmed the moral indifference of human acts when he declared, 'We are no guiltier in following the primitive impulses that govern us than is the Nile for her floods or the sea for her waves.' Similarly, Sade, in order to excuse himself, compares himself to plants, animals, and the elements. 'In her hands I am only a tool that she [Nature] manipulates as she pleases.' Although he constantly took refuge in similar statements, they do not express his real thoughts. In the first place, Nature, for him, is not an indifferent mechanism. There is such significance in her transformations that one might play with the idea that she is governed by an evil genius. Nature is actually cruel and voracious, informed with the spirit of destruction. She 'would desire the utter annihilation of all living creatures so as to enjoy her power of recreating new ones.' However, man is not her slave.

Sade had already pointed out in *Aline et Valcour* that he can wrest himself free and turn against her. 'Let us dare do violence to this unintelligible Nature, the better to master the art of enjoying her.' And he declared even more decisively in *Juliette*, 'Once man is created, he is no longer dependent upon Nature; once Nature has launched him, she has no further hold on him.' He goes further. Man, in his relation to Nature, is comparable to 'the froth, the vapor which rises from the rarefied liquid in a heated vessel. The vapor is not created; it is a resultant; it is heterogeneous. It derives its existence from a foreign element. It can exist or not, without detriment to the element from which it issues. It owes nothing to the element and the element owes nothing to it.' Though man is of no more value to the universe than a bit of froth, it is this very insignificance which guarantees his autonomy. The natural order cannot control him since he is radically alien to it.

Hence, he may make a moral decision, and no one has the right to dictate to him. Why then, with all the paths open to him, did Sade choose the one which led, through the imitation of Nature, to crime? To answer this question, we must understand his system in its totality; the aim of this system was precisely to justify the 'crimes' which Sade never dreamed of renouncing.

We are always more influenced than we realize by the ideas we fight against. To be sure, Sade often uses naturalism as an *ad nominem* argument. He took sly pleasure in turning to evil account the examples which his contemporaries tried to exploit on behalf of the Good, but no doubt he also took for granted that might makes right. When he tries to demonstrate the fact that the libertine has the right to oppress women, he exclaims, 'Has not Nature proved, in giving us the strength necessary to submit them to our desires, that we have the right to do so?' One could find many similar quotations. 'Nature has made us all equal at birth, Sophie,' says La Dubois to Justine, 'If Nature wishes to disturb this first stage of general laws, it is for us to correct her caprices.' Sade's basic charge against the codes imposed by society is that they are artificial. He compares them, in a particularly significant text, to those that might be drawn up by a community of blind men.[11] 'All those duties are imaginary, since they are only conventional. In like manner, man has made laws relative to his petty knowledge, his petty wiles, and his petty needs – but all this has no reality. . . . When we look at Nature we readily understand that everything we decide and organize is as far removed from the perfection of her views and as inferior to her as the laws of the society of blind men would be to our own.'

Montesquieu had advanced the idea that laws were dependent on climate, circumstances, and even the arrangement of the 'fibers' of our bodies. It might be concluded that they express the various aspects assumed by Nature in time and space. But the indefatigable Sade takes us to Tahiti, Patagonia, and the antipodes, to show us that the diversity of enacted laws definitively negates their value. Though they may be related, they seem to him arbitrary. And it should be noted that for him the words 'conventional' and 'imaginary' are synonymous. Nature retains her sacred character for Sade: indivisible and unique, she is an absolute, outside of which there is no reality.

It is obvious that Sade's thinking on this point was not quite coherent, that it was not at all times equally sincere, and that it was constantly developing. But his inconsistencies are not quite

[11] *Pensée* printed by Maurice Heine, *Le Marquis de Sade* (Paris, 1950). See below pp. 146-149.

so obvious as one might think. The syllogism: Nature is evil, and therefore the society that departs from Nature merits our obedience, is far too simple. In the first place, society is suspect because of its hypocrisy. It appeals to Nature's authority even though it is really hostile to her. And besides, society is rooted in Nature, despite its antagonism to her. Society manifests its original perversion by the very way in which it contradicts Nature. The idea of general interest has no natural basis. 'The interests of individuals are almost always opposed to those of society.' But the idea was invented in order to satisfy a natural instinct, namely, the tyrannical will of the strong. Laws, instead of correcting the primitive order of the world, only aggravate its injustice. 'We are are all alike, except in strength,' that is, there are no essential differences among individuals, and the unequal distribution of strength might have been offset. Instead, the strong have arrogated to themselves all the forms of superiority and have even invented others.

Holbach, and many others along with him, had exposed the hypocrisy of codes whose sole purpose was to oppress the weak. Morelly and Brissot, among others, had shown that the ownership of property has no natural basis. Society has fabricated this harmful institution out of whole cloth. 'There is no exclusive ownership in Nature,' wrote Brissot. 'The word has been struck from her code. The unhappy starveling may carry off and devour his bread because he is hungry. His claim is his hunger.' In *La Philosophie dans le Boudoir* Sade uses almost the same terms to demand that the idea of possession be substituted for that of proprietorship. How can proprietorship claim to be a universally recognized right when the poor rebel against it and the rich dream only of increasing it by further monopolizing? 'It is by complete equality of wealth and condition and not by vain laws that the power of the stronger must be weakened.' But the fact is that it is the strong who make the laws for their own profit.

Their presumptuousness is odiously apparent in their arrogation of the right to inflict punishment. Beccaria had maintained that the aim of punishment was to procure redress, but that no one could claim the right to punish. Sade indignantly spoke out against all penalties of an expiatory character. 'Oh, slaughterers, gaolers, and imbeciles of all regimes and governments, when will you come to prefer the science of understanding man to that of imprisoning and killing him?' He rebels particularly against the death penalty. Society tries to justify it by the *lex talionis*, but this is just another fantasy without roots in reality. In the first place, there is no reciprocity among the subjects; their existences

46

are not commensurable. Nor is there any similarity between a murder committed in a burst of passion or out of need, and coldly premeditated assassination by judges. And how can the latter in any way compensate for the former? In erecting scaffolds, society, far from mitigating the cruelty of Nature, merely aggravates it. Actually, it resists evil by doing greater evil. Its claim on our loyalty is without foundation.

The famous contract invoked by Hobbes and Rousseau is just a myth; how could individual freedom be recognized in an order that oppresses it? This pact is to the interest of neither the strong, who have nothing to gain in abdicating their privileges, nor the weak, whose inferiority is thereby confirmed. There can be only a state of war between these two groups; and each has its own values, which are irreconcilable with those of the other. 'When he took a hundred louis from a man's pocket, he was committing what was for him a just act, though the man who had been robbed must have regarded it quite otherwise.' In the speech which he puts into the mouth of Coeur de Fer, Sade passionately exposes the bourgeois hoax which consists in erecting class interests into universal principles. Since the concrete conditions under which individuals live are not homogeneous, no universal morality is possible.

But ought we not to try to reform society, since it has betrayed its own aspirations? Cannot individual freedom be put precisely to this use? It seems not improbable that Sade may at times have envisaged this solution. It is significant that in *Aline et Valcour* he describes with equal indulgence the anarchic society of cannibals and the communistic society of Zamé in which evil is disarmed by justice. I do not think there that is any irony at all in the latter picture, any more than in the appeal, 'Frenchmen! A further effort'[12] inserted into *La Philosophie dans le Boudoir*. Sade's activity during the Revolution clearly proves that he wished to be integrated into a collectivity. He suffered bitterly from the ostracism to which he was subjected.

He dreamed of an ideal society from which his special tastes would not exclude him. He really thought that such tastes would not constitute a serious danger to an enlightened society. Zamé assures us that he would not be disturbed by Sade's disciples: 'The people you speak of are few; they do not worry me at all.' And Sade, in a letter, maintains: 'It is not the opinions or vices of private individuals that are harmful to the state, but rather the behavior

[12] It has been maintained that Sade does not endorse this statement since he puts it into the mouth of the Chevalier. But the Chevalier merely reads a text of which Dolmancé, Sade's mouthpiece, admits he is the author. See below pp. 90-115.

of public figures.' The fact is that the libertine's acts have no real influence; they are not much more than games. Sade takes refuge behind their insignificance and goes so far as to suggest that he would be ready to sacrifice them. Motivated as they are by defiance and resentment, these acts would lose their significance in a world without hatred. If the prohibitions which make crime attractive were abolished, lust itself would be eliminated. Perhaps Sade really longed for the personal conversion that would result from the conversion of other men. He probably expected, also, that his vices would be accepted as something exceptional by a community which respected singularity and which would, therefore, recognize him as an exception. He was sure, in any case, that a man who was content with whipping a prostitute every now and then was less harmful to society than a farmer-general.

The real plagues are established injustice, official abuses, and constitutional crimes; and these are the inevitable accompaniments of abstract laws which try to impose themselves uniformly upon a plurality of radically separate objects. A just economic order would render codes and courts useless, for crime is born of need and illegality and would vanish with the elimination of these grounds. The ideal regime, for Sade, was a kind of reasonable anarchy: 'The reign of law is inferior to that of anarchy. The greatest proof of what I advance is to be found in the fact that all governments are obliged to plunge into anarchy when they wish to remake their constitutions. In order to abrogate its old laws, a government is obliged to establish a revolutionary regime in which there are no laws. New laws are ultimately born of this regime, but this second state is nevertheless less pure than the first, since it is derived from it.' This argument probably does not sound very convincing, but what Sade understood remarkably well was that the ideology of his time was merely the expression of an economic system and that a concrete transformation of this system would put an end to the humbug of bourgeois morality. Very few of his contemporaries developed such penetrating views in such an *extreme* way.

Nevertheless, Sade did not definitely take the path of social reform. His life and work were not guided by these utopian reveries. How could he have gone on believing in them very long in the depths of his dungeon cells or after the Terror? Events confirmed his private experience. Society's failure was no mere accident. And besides, it was obvious that his interest in its possible success was of a purely speculative nature. He was obsessed by his own case. He cared little about changing himself and much more about being confirmed in his choices. His vices condemned

48

him to solitude. He was to demonstrate the necessity of solitude and the supremacy of evil. It was easy for him to be honest because, maladjusted aristocrat that he was, he had never encountered men like himself. Though he mistrusted generalizations, he ascribed to his situation the value of a metaphysical inevitability: 'Man is isolated in the world.' 'All creatures are born isolated and have no need of one another.' If the diversty of human beings could be assimilated – as Sade himself frequently suggests – to that which differentiates plants or animals, a reasonable society would manage to surmount it. It would be enough merely to respect each one's particularity.

But man does not merely undergo his solitude; he demands it *against everyone*. It follows that there is a heterogeneity of values, not only from class to class, but from individual to individual. 'All passions have two meanings, Juliette: one, which is very unjust as regards the victim; the other, which is singularly just to the person who exercises it. And this fundamental antagonism cannot be transcended because it is the truth itself.' If human projects tried to reconcile themselves in a common quest for the general interest, they would be necessarily inauthentic. For there is no reality other than that of the self-enclosed subject hostile to any other subject which disputes its sovereignty. The thing that prevents individual freedom from choosing Good is that the latter does not not exist in the empty sky or the unjust earth or even at some ideal horizon; it is nowhere to be found. Evil is an absolute resisted only by fanciful notions, and there is only one way of asserting oneself in the face of it: to assent to it.

For there is one idea that Sade, throughout his pessimism, savagely rejects: the idea of submission. And that is why he detests the hypocritical resignation which is adorned with the name of virtue. It is a stupid submission to the rule of evil, as recreated by society. In submitting, a man renounces both his authenticity and his freedom. It was easy for Sade to show that chastity and temperance are not even justified by their usefulness. The prejudices that condemn incest, sodomy, and all sexual *vagaries* have but one aim: to destroy the individual by imposing upon him a stupid conformism. But the great virtues extolled by the age had a deeper meaning; they tried to palliate the all too obvious inadequacies of the law. Sade raised no objection to tolerance, probably because, so far as he could observe, no one even tried to practice it; but he did attack fanatically what is called humaneness and benevolence. These were mystifications which aimed at reconciling the irreconcilable: the unsatisfied appetites of the poor and the selfish greed of the rich. Taking up the tradition of La Rochefoucauld, he shows that these are merely masks to disguise self-interest.

The weak, in order to check the arrogance of the strong, have invented the idea of fraternity, an idea which has no solid basis: 'Now I beg of you to tell me whether I must love a human being simply because he exists or resembles me and whether for these reasons alone I must suddenly prefer him to myself?' What hypocrisy on the part of privileged persons who make a great to-do about their philanthrophy and at the same time acquiesce in the object condition of the poor! This false sentimentality was so widespread at the time that even Valmont, in *Les Liaisons Dangereuses*, was moved to tears when he performed an act of charity; and it was obviously the currency of this mode of feeling that made Sade unleash all his dishonesty and sincerity against *benevolence*. He is certainly joking when he claims that in maltreating prostitutes he is serving the cause of morality. If libertines were permitted to molest them with impunity, prostitution would become so dangerous a profession that no one would engage in it. But he is quite right in cutting through sophisms and exposing the inconsistencies of a society that protects the very things it condemns, and which, though permitting debauchery, often punishes the debauchee.

He reveals the dangers of almsgiving with the same somber irony. If the poor are not reduced to hopelessness, they may rebel; and the safest thing would be to exterminate all of them. In this scheme, which he attributes to Saint-Fond, Sade develops the idea in Swift's famous pamphlet, and he certainly does not identify himself with his hero. Nevertheless, the cynicism of this aristocrat, who fully espoused the interests of his class, is more valid to him than the compromises of guilty-minded hedonists. His thinking is clear – either do away with the poor or do away with poverty, but do not use half-measures and thus perpetuate injustice and oppression,[13] and above all do not pretend to be redeeming these extortions by handing out a trivial dole to those you exploit. If Sade's heroes let some poor wretch die of hunger rather than defile themselves by an act of charity that would cost them nothing, it is because they passionately refuse any complicity with respectable people who appease their consciences so cheaply.

Virtue deserves no admiration and no gratitude since, far from reflecting the demands of a transcendant good, it serves the interests of those who make a show of it. It is only logical that Sade should come to this conclusion. But after all, if self-interest is

---

[13] This policy of all or nothing is found among present-day Communists. They repudiate bourgeois charity; and there are many who, on principle, refuse any private help to the needy.

the individual's sole law, why despise it? In what respect is it inferior to vice? Sade answered this question often and vehemently. In cases where virtue is chosen, he says, 'What lack of movement! What ice! Nothing stirs me, nothing excites me . . . I ask you, is this pleasure? What a difference on the other side! What tickling of my senses! What excitement in my organs!' And again: 'Happiness lies only in that which excites and the only thing that excites is crime.' In terms of the hedonism of his time, this argument carries weight. The only objection one might make is that Sade generalizes from his own individual case. May not some people be excited also by the good? He rejects this eclecticism. *Virtue can procure only an imaginary happiness;* 'true felicity lies only in the senses, and virtue gratifies none of them.' This statement may seem surprising, since Sade had actually made the imagination the mainspring of vice; but vice teaches us a certain truth through the very fantasies on which it feeds, and the proof is that it ends in orgasm, that is, in a definite sensation; whereas the illusions on which virtue feeds are never concretely recouped by the individual. According to the philosophy that Sade borrowed from his age, sensation is the only measure of reality, and if virtue arouses no sensation, it is because it has no real basis.

Sade explains what he means more clearly in the following parallel between virtue and vice: 'The first is chimerical; the other is real. The one is based on prejudices; the other, on reason. If . . . from one; I feel hardly anything from the other.' Virtue, chimercal and imaginary, encloses us in a world of appearances; whereas vice's intimate link with the flesh guarantees its genuineness. Using the vocabulary of Stirner, whose name has rightly been linked with Sade's, we might say that virtue alienates the individual from that empty entity, Man. It is only in crime that he justifies and fulfills himself as a concrete ego. If poor man resigns himself or vainly tries to fight for his fellows, he is maneuvered and duped, an inert object, a plaything of Nature; he is nothing. He must, like La Dubois or Coeur de Fer, try to pass over to the side of the strong. The rich person who accepts his privileges passively also exists like an object. If he abuses his power and becomes a tyrant, then he is someone. Instead of losing himself in philanthropic dreams, he will cynically take advantage of the injustice that favors him. 'Where would be the victims of our villainy if all men were criminals? We must never cease to keep the people tied to the yoke of error and the lie,' says Esterval.

Are we back to the idea that man can only act in obedience to his evil nature? Is he not destroying his freedom with the pretext of safeguarding his authenticity? No, for though freedom may be unable to go counter to given reality, it is able to wrest itself away from it and assume it. This procedure is similar to Stoic conversion which, by deliberate decision, turns reality to its own account. There is no contradiction in Sade's extolling crime and at the same time getting indignant about men's injustice, selfishness, and cruelty.[14] He has only contempt for the timid vices, for the rash crimes which merely reflect passively the heinousness of Nature. One must *make oneself* a criminal in order to avoid *being* evil, as is a volcano or a member of the police. It is not a matter of submitting to the universe, but of imitating it in open defiance.

This is the attitude that Almani, the chemist, assumes at the edge of Mount Etna. 'Yes, my friend, yes, I abhor Nature. And the reason I loathe her is that I know her all too well. Knowing her dreadful secrets, I felt a kind of ineffable pleasure in copying her heinousness. I shall imitate her, though I hate her. . . . Her murderous nets are spread for us alone. Let us try to catch her in her own trap. . . . In presenting to me only her effects, she concealed all her causes. I am therefore limited to imitating the former. Unable to guess the motive that put the dagger into her hands, I have been able to take away her weapon and use it as she did.' This text has the same ambiguous ring as the words of Dolmancé: 'It was their ingratitude that dried up my heart.' It reminds us that it was in despair and resentment that Sade devoted himself to evil. And it is in this respect that his hero is distinguished from the ancient sage. He does not follow Nature lovingly and joyously. He copies her with abhorrence and without understanding her. And he wills himself to be something without approving himself. Evil is not at one with itself; self-laceration is its very essence.

This laceration must be experienced in a state of constant tension; otherwise, it congeals into remorse and, as such, constitutes a mortal danger. Blanchot has observed that whenever the Sadistic hero, as a result of some scruple, restores to society its power over him, he is doomed to the worst kind of catastrophe. Repentance and hesitation mean that one recognizes that one has judges. It therefore means accepting guilt instead of assuming that one is the free author of one's acts. The man who consents to to his passivity deserves all the defeats that the hostile world will inflict upon him. On the other hand: 'The genuine libertine likes even the charges that are leveled against him for his execrable crimes. Have we not known men who loved even the tortures appointed by human vengeance, who suffered them gladly, who

---

[14] The similarity with Stirner at this point is striking. Stirner also condemns 'vulgar' crime and extols only that which makes for the fulfillment of the ego.

looked upon the scaffold as a throne of glory? These are men who have attained the highest degree of deliberate corruption.'

At this ultimate degree, man is delivered not only of prejudices and shame, but of fear as well. His serenity is that of the ancient sage who regarded as futile 'things which do not depend on ourselves.' But the sage confined himself to a completely negative self-defense against possible suffering. The dark stoicism of Sade promises positive happiness. Thus, Coeur de Fer lays down the following alternatives: 'Either the crime which makes us happy, or the scaffold which prevents us from being unhappy.' Nothing can threaten the man who can transform his very defeats into triumphs. He fears nothing because for him everything is good. The brutal factitiousness of things does not crush the free man because it does not interest him. He is concerned only with their meaning, and the meaning depends only upon him. A person who is whipped or penetrated by another may be the other's master as well as his slave. The ambivalence of pain and pleasure, of humiliation and pride, enables the libertine to dominate any situation. Thus, Juliette can transform into pleasure the same tortures that prostrate Justine, Fundamentally, the content of the experience is unimportant. The thing that counts is the subject's intention.

Thus, hedonism ends in ataraxia, which confirms the paradoxical relation between sadism and stoicism. The individual's promised happiness is reduced to indifference. 'I have been happy, my dear, ever since I have been indulging cold-bloodedly in every sort of crime,' says Bressac. Cruelty appears in a new light, as an *ascesis*. 'The man who can grow callous to the pains of others becomes insensitive to his own.' It is no longer excitement we must seek, but *apathy*. A budding libertine, no doubt, needs violent emotions in order to feel the truth of his individual existence. But once he has possessed it, the pure form of crime will be enough to ensure it. Crime has 'a character of grandeur and sublimity which prevails and always will prevail over the dull charms of virtue' and which renders vain all the contingent satisfactions one might be tempted to expect. With a severity similar to Kant's, and which has its source in the same puritan tradition, Sade conceives the free act only as an act free of all feeling. If it were to obey emotional motives, it would make us Nature's slaves again and not autonomous subjects.

This choice is open to any individual, regardless of his situation. One of the victims locked up in the monk's harem where Justine is languishing away manages to escape her fate by proving her worth. She stabs one of her companions with a viciousness that arouses the admiration of her masters and makes her the queen of the harem. Those who remain among the oppressed do so because they are poor-spirited, and they must not be pitied. 'What can there possibly be in common between the man who can do everything and the one who doesn't dare do anything?' The contrast of the two words is significant. For Sade, if one dares, one can. Blanchot has commented upon the austerity of this morality. Almost all of Sade's criminals die violent deaths, and it is their merit that transforms their misfortunes into glory. But in fact, death is not the worst of failures, and whatever the fate Sade reserves for his heroes, he assures them a destiny which allows them to fulfill themselves. This optimism comes from an aristocratic vision of mankind, which involves, in its implacable severity, a doctrine of predestination.

For this quality of mind which enables a few elect spirits to rule over a herd of condemned souls appears as an arbitrary dispensation of grace. Juliette was saved and Justine lost from the beginning of time. Even more interesting is the view that merit cannot entail success unless it is *recognized*. The strength of mind of Valérie and Juliette would have been to no avail had it not deserved the admiration of their tyrants. Divided and separated though they be, it must be admitted that they do bow down together before certain values, and they choose reality in the different guises which for Sade are, without question, equivalent to one another: orgasm – nature – reason. Or, to be more precise, reality imposes itself upon them. The hero triumphs through their mediation. But what saves him finally is the fact that he has staked everything on the truth. Sade believes in an absolute which is beyond all contingencies and which can never disappoint the one who invokes it as a last resort.

It is only out of pusillanimity that everyone does not embrace such a sure ethic, for there can be no vaild objection to it. It cannot offend a God who is a mere figment of the imagination; and since Nature is essentially division and hostility, to attack her is to conform to her all the more. Yielding to his naturalistic prejudices, Sade writes, 'The only real crime would be to outrage Nature,' and adds immediately afterward, 'Is it conceivable that Nature would provide us with the possibility of a crime that would outrage her?' She takes unto herself everything that happens. She even receives murder with indifference, since 'the life principle of all creatures is death; this death is merely a matter of imagination. Only a man attaches importance to his own existence, but he 'could completely wipe out his species without the universe's feeling the slightest change.' He claims to have a sacred character which makes him untouchable, but he is only one animal among

54

others. 'Only man's pride has made a crime of murder.'

Indeed, Sade's plea is so forceful that he ends by denying any criminal character to crime. He realizes this himself. The last part of *Juliette* is a convulsive attempt to rekindle the flame of Evil, but despite volcanoes, fires, poison, and plague, if there is no God, man is merely smoke. If Nature permits everything, then the worst catastrophes are a matter of indifference. 'To my mind, man's greatest torment is the impossibility of offending Nature!' And if Sade had staked everything only on the demoniacal horror of crime, his ethic would have ended in radical failure; but if he himself accepted this defeat, it was only because he was fighting for something else, namely, his profound conviction that crime is good.

In the first place, crime is not only inoffensive to Nature; it is useful to her. Sade explains in *Juliette* that if 'the spirit of the three kingdoms' were confronted with no obstacles, it would get so violent that it would paralyze the working of the universe. 'There would be neither gravitation nor movement.' As a result of its inner contradiction, human crimes save it from the stagnation which would also endanger an overly virtuous society. Sade had certainly read Mandeville's *The Grumbling Hive* which had had a great success at the beginning of the eighteenth century. Mandeville had shown that the passions and defects of individuals served the public welfare and even that the greatest scoundrels were the ones who worked most actively for the common good. When an inopportune conversion made for the triumph of virtue, the hive was ruined. Sade also declared repeatedly that a collectivity that *fell* into virtue would thereby be pushed into inertia. We have here a kind of presage of the Hegelian theory according to which 'the spirit's restlessness' could not be abolished without involving the end of history. But, for Sade, immobility appears not as a static plenitude but as a pure absence. Mankind makes every effort by means of the conventions with which it is armed to cut all its ties with Nature; and it would become a pale phantom were it not for a few resolute souls who maintain within it, in spite of itself, the rights of truth – and truth means discord, war, and agitation.

In the strange text where he compares us all to blind men,[15] Sade says that it is already enough that our limited senses prevent us from attaining the core of reality. Let us, therefore, not spoil our pleasure even more. Let us try to transcend our limits: 'The most perfect being we could conceive would be the one who alienated himself most from our conventions and found them

[15] See below pp. 146-149.

most contemptible.' In its proper context, this statement recalls both Rimbaud's demand for a 'systematic derangement' of all the senses and the attempts of the surrealists to penetrate beyond human artifice to the mysterious heart of the real. But it is as moralist rather than as poet that Sade tries to shatter the prison of appearances. The mystified and mystifying society against which he rebels suggests Heidegger's 'the one' in which the authenticity of existence is swallowed up. For Sade, too, it is a question of regaining authenticity by an individual decision. These comparisons are quite deliberate. Sade must be given a place in the great family of those who want to cut through the 'banality of everyday life' to a truth which is immanent in this world. Within this framework, crime becomes a duty: 'In a criminal society one must be a criminal.' This formula sums up his ethic. By means of crime, the libertine refuses any complicity with the evils of the given situation, of which the masses are merely the passive, and hence abject, reflection. It prevents society from reposing in injustice and creates an apocalyptic condition which constrains all individuals to ensure their separateness, and thus their truth, in a state of constant tension.

Nevertheless, it is in the name of the individual that it seems possible to raise the most convincing objections to Sade's notions; for the individual is quite real, and crime does him real injury. It is here that Sade's thinking proves to be *extreme*: the only thing that has truth for me is that which is enveloped in my own experience; the inner presence of other people is foreign to me. Hence, it does not concern me and cannot dictate any duty to me. 'We don't care a bit about the torment of others; what have we in common with this torment?' And again: 'There is no comparison between what others experience and what we feel. The strongest pain in other people is certainly nothing to us, but we are affected by the slightest tickle of pleasure that touches us.' The fact is that the only sure bonds among men are those they create in transcending themselves into another world by means of common projects. The only project that the hedonistic sensualism of the eighteenth century has to offer the individual is to 'procure pleasant sensations and feelings.' It fixes him in his lonely immanence. Sade shows us in *Justine* a surgeon who plans to dissect his daughter in order to further science and thereby mankind. Seen in terms of its transcendent future, mankind has value in his eyes; but what is a man when reduced to his mere vain presence? Just a pure fact, stripped of all value, who affects me no more than a lifeless stone. 'My neighbor is nothing to me; there is not the slightest relationship between him and myself.'

56

These statements seem contradictory to Sade's attitude in real life. It is obvious that if there were nothing in *common* between the tortures of the victims and the torturer, the latter would derive no pleasure from them. But what Sade is actually disputing is the a priori existence of a given relationship between myself and the other by which my behavior should be guided in the abstract. He does not deny the possibility of establishing such a relationship; and if he rejects ethical recognition of other people founded on false notions of reciprocity and universality, it is in order to give himself the authority to destroy the concrete barriers of flesh which isolate human minds. Each mind bears witness only for itself as to the value it attributes to itself and has no right to impose this value upon others. But it can, in a singular and vivid manner, demand recognition of such value in its acts. This is the course chosen by the criminal, who, by the violence of his self-assertion, becomes real for the other person and thereby also reveals the other as really existing. But it should be noted that, quite unlike the conflict described by Hegel, this process involves no risk for the subject. His primacy is not at stake; regardless of what happens to him, he will accept no master. If he is defeated, he returns to a solitude which ends in death, but he remains sovereign.

Thus, for the despot, other people do not represent a danger that could strike at the heart of his being. Nevertheless, this outside world from which he is excluded irritates him. He wants to penetrate it. Paradoxically enough, he is free to make things happen in this forbidden domain, and the temptation is all the more dizzying in that these events will be incommensurable with his experience. Sade repeatedly stresses the point that it is not the unhappiness of the other person which excites the libertine, but rather the knowledge that he is responsible for it. This is something very different from an abstract deomoniacal pleasure. When he weaves his dark plots, he sees his freedom being transformed for others into a destiny. And as death is more certain than life, and suffering more certain than happiness, it is in persecutions and murder that he takes unto himself this mystery. But it is not enough to impose oneself upon the bewildered victim in the guise of destiny. Duped and mystified as he is, one possesses him, but only from without. In revealing himself to the victim, the torturer incites him to manifest his freedom in his screams or prayers. If it is not revealed, the victim is unworthy of torture. One kills him or forgets about him. He may also escape his torturer by the violence of his revolt, be it flight, suicide, or victory. What the torturer demands is that, alternating between refusal and submission, whether rebelling or consenting, the victim recognize, in any case

57

that his destiny is the freedom of the tyrant. He is then united to his tyrant by the closest of bonds. They form a genuine couple.

There are occasional cases in which the victim's freedom, without escaping the destiny which the tyrant creates for it, succeeds in getting around it. It turns suffering into pleasure, shame into pride; it becomes an accomplice. It is then that the debauchee is gratified to the full: 'There is no keener pleasure for a libertine mind than to win proselytes.' To debauch an innocent creature is obviously a satanic act; but in view of the ambivalence of evil, we effect a genuine conversion by winning for it a new adept. The capturing of a virginity, among other things, appears in this light as a ceremony of initiation. Just as we must outrage Nature in order to imitate her, though the outrage is canceled out since she herself demands it, so, in doing violence to an individual, we force him to assume his separateness and thereby he finds a truth which reconciles him with his antagonist. Torturer and victim recognize their fellowship in astonishment, esteem, and even admiration.

It has rightly been pointed out that there is never any permanent bond among Sade's libertines, that their relationship involves a constant tension. But the fact that Sade systematically makes selfishness triumph over friendship does not prevent him from endowing friendship with reality. Noirceuil is very careful to let Juliette know that he is interested in her only because of the pleasure he finds in her company; but this pleasure implies a concrete relationship between them. Each feels confirmed within himself by the presence of an alter ego; it is both an absolution and an exaltation. Group debauchery produces genuine communion among Sade's libertines. Each one perceives the meaning of his acts and of his own figure through the minds of the others. I experience my own flesh in the flesh of another; then my fellow creature really exists for me. The shocking fact of coexistence eludes our thinking, but we can dispose of its mystery the way Alexander cut through the Gordian knot; we must set ourselves down in it by acts. 'What an enigma is man! – Yes, my friend, and that's what made a very witty man say that it's better to f . . . him than to understand him.' Eroticism appears in Sade as a mode of communication, the only valid one. We might say, parodying Claudel, that in Sade 'the penis is the shortest path between two hearts.'

To sympathize with Sade too readily is to betray him. For it is our misery, subjection, and death that he desires; and every time we side with a child whose throat has been slit by a sex-maniac, we take a stand against him. Nor does he forbid us to defend ourselves. He allows that a father may revenge or prevent, even by murder,

58

the rape of his child. What he demands is that, in the struggle between irreconcilable existences, each one engage himself concretely in the name of his own existence. He approves of the vendetta, but not of the courts. We may kill, but we may not judge. The pretensions of the judge are more arrogant than those of the tyrant; for the tyrant confines himself to being himself, whereas the judge tries to erect his opinions into universal laws. His effort is based upon a lie. For every person is imprisoned in his own skin and cannot become the mediator between separate persons from whom he himself is separated. And the fact that a great number of these individuals band together and alienate themselves in institutions, of which they are no longer masters, gives them no additional right. Their number has nothing to do with the matter. There is no way of measuring the incommensurable. In order to escape the conflicts of existence, we take refuge in a universe of appearances, and existence itself escapes us. In thinking that we are defending ourselves, we are destroying ourselves. Sade's immense merit lies in his taking a stand against these abstractions and alienations which are merely flights from the truth about man. No one was more passionately attached to the concrete than he. He never respected the 'everyone says' with which mediocre minds lazily content themselves. He adhered only to the truths which were derived from the evidence of his own actual experience. Thus, he went beyond the sensualism of his age and transformed it into an ethic of authenticity.

This does not mean that we can be satisfied with the solution he offers. For if Sade's desires to grasp the very essence of the human condition in terms of his particular situation is the source of his greatness, it is also responsible for his limits. He thought that the solution he chose for himself was valid for everyone else, to the exclusion of any other. Wherein he was doubly mistaken. For all his pessimism, he was, socially, on the side of the privileged, and he did not understand that social injustice affects the individual even in his ethical potentialities. Even rebellion is a luxury requiring culture, leisure, and a certain detachment from the needs of existence. Though Sade's heroes may pay with their lives for such rebellion, at least they do so after it has given their lives a valid meaning; whereas for the great majority of men it would be tantamount to a stupid suicide. Contrary to his wishes, it is chance, and not merit, which would operate in the selection of a criminal elite. If it is objected that he never strove for universality, that he wanted only to ensure his own salvation – that does not do him justice. He offers himself as an example, since he wrote – and so passionately! – of his own experience. And he probably did not expect his appeal to be heard by everyone. But he did not think that he was addressing only the members of the privileged classes, whose arrogance he detested. The kind of predestination in which he believed was democratically conceived, and he would not have wanted to discover that it depended upon the economic circumstances from which, as he saw it, it should allow one to escape.

Moreover, he did not suppose that there could be any possible way other than individual rebellion. He knew only two alternatives: abstract morality and crime. He was unaware of action. Though he might have suspected the possibility of a concrete communication among subjects through an undertaking which might unite all men in the common realization of their manhood, he did not stop there. Denying the individual all transcendence, he consigns him to an insignificance which authorizes his violation. But this violence in the void becomes absurd, and the tyrant who tries to assert himself by such violence discovers merely his own nothingness.

To this contradiction, however, Sade might oppose another. For the eighteenth century's fond dream of reconciling individuals within their immanence is, in any case, unfeasible. Sade embodied in his own way his disappointment with the Terror. The individual who is unwilling to deny his particularity is repudiated by society. But if we choose to recognize in each subject only the transcendence which unites him concretely with his fellows, we are leading him only to new idols, and their particular insignificance will appear all the more obvious. We shall be sacrificing today to tomorrow, the minority to the majority, the freedom of each to the achievements of the community. Prison and the guillotine will be the logical consequences of this denial. The illusory brotherhood ends in crimes, wherein virtue recognizes her abstract features. 'Nothing resembles virtue more than a great crime,' said Saint-Just is it not better to assume the burden of evil than to subscribe to this abstract good which drags in its wake abstract slaughters? It is probably impossible to escape this dilemma. If the entire human population of the earth were present to each individual in its full reality, no collective action would be possible, and the air would become unbreathable for everyone. Thousands of individuals are suffering and dying vainly and unjustly at every moment, and this does not affect us. If it did, our existence would be impossible. Sade's merit lies not only in his having proclaimed aloud what everyone admits with shame to himself, but in the fact that he did not simply resign himself. He chose cruelty rather than indifference. This is probably why he finds so many echoes today, when the individual knows that he is more the victim of men's good consciences than of their wickedness. To unleash this terrifying optimism is to come to his aid. In the solitude of his prison cells, Sade lived through an ethical darkness similar to the intellectual night in which Descartes wrapped himself. He emerged with no revelation, but at least he disputed all the easy answers. If ever we hope to transcend the separateness of individuals, we may do so only on condition that we be aware of its existence. Otherwise, promises of happiness and justice conceal the worst dangers. Sade drained to the dregs the moment of selfishness, injustice, and misery, and he insisted upon its truth. The supreme value of his testimony is the fact that it disturbs us. It forces us to re-examine thoroughly the basic problem which haunts our age in different forms: the true relation between man and man.

PART II

*Selections from the Writings of
The Marquis de Sade*

DIALOGUE
BETWEEN A PRIEST AND A DYING MAN

PRIEST: Come to this fatal moment when the veil of illusion is torn away, only to leave deluded man with the remorseful picture of his errors and vices, do you not, my child, repent of the many evils that human weakness and frailty have led you to?

DYING MAN: Yes, my friend, I do repent.

PRIEST: Then take advantage of this opportune remorse to secure from heaven, in the brief space of time left you, general absolution from your sins, and bear in mind that it is only by means of the most holy sacrament of penance that it will be possible for you to obtain it from the Lord.

DYING MAN: I no more understand you than you have understood me.

PRIEST: What!

DYING MAN: I told you that I repented.

PRIEST: I heard you say so.

DYING MAN: Yes, but without understanding.

PRIEST: What interpretation?

DYING MAN: This. . . . Created by Nature with keen tastes and strong passions, uniquely situated in this world to indulge and satisfy them. . . . I only repent of not having sufficiently recognized her omnipotence; and my sole regrets are only of the indifferent use I made of the faculties – criminal in your eyes, but natural in mine – she endowed me with to serve her. At times I have resisted, and that I regret. Blinded by the absurdities of your creed, I used it to fight the whole onrush of desire that came to me by an inspiration far more divine; and I regret it. I have gathered only flowers when I might have made an abundant harvest of fruits. These are the true reasons for my sorrows; deem me wise enough not to suppose any others in me.

PRIEST: See to what your errors drag you! Where your sophisms lead you! You endow the thing created with all the potentiality of the Creator, and you do not see that these unhappy tastes that have led you astray are only the effects of this corrupted Nature to which you attribute omnipotence.

DYING MAN: My friend, it seems to me that your dialectics are as false as your thoughts. I would like you either to reason more accurately or to let me die in peace. What do you mean by 'creator,' and what do you mean by 'corrupted nature'?

PRIEST: The Creator is the lord of the universe, it is He who has made all things, created all, and who keeps all simply by the working of His omnipotence.

DYING MAN: There's a great man, to be sure . . . But tell me, why has this man who is so powerful made, according to you, a corrupted Nature?

PRIEST: What merit should men have, if God had not left them their free will? And what worthiness in enjoying it if on earth there were not the possibility of doing good and shunning evil?

DYING MAN: So your God would make everything awry just to tempt or to try His creature? Did He not know him then? Had He not any doubts as to the result?

PRIEST: Doubtless He did know him, but once again, He wished to leave him the credit of choosing.

DYING MAN: To what good end, since He knew the side he would take, and it only depended on Him, since you said He was omnipotent, it only depended on Him to make him take the good?

PRIEST: Who can comprehend the vast and infinite designs of God upon man, and who can understand all we see?

DYING MAN: The man who simplifies things, my friend, and especially the man who does not increase the causes the better to muddle the effects. What do you want with a second difficulty when you cannot explain the first? And since it is possible that Nature quite unaided has done all that you attribute to your God, why do you want to look for a master for her? The cause you fail to understand is perhaps the simplest thing in the world. Bring your body to perfection and you will understand Nature better. Refine your reasoning, expel your prejudices, and you will no longer need your God.

PRIEST: Do you not believe in God at all?

DYING MAN: No. And for a very plain reason, which is that it is completely impossible to believe what one does not understand.

* * *

PRIEST: But in the end you must acknowledge something after this life. It is impossible that your thoughts have not at times been pleased to penetrate the deep shadows of the fate that awaits us; and what creed can better satisfy it than that which sees infinite punishment for the man who lives evilly and an eternity of rewards for the man who lives the good life?

DYING MAN: What one, my friend? That of nothingness, because it has never frightened me, and in it I see nothing but consolation

66

and naturalness. All others are the work of pride, and this alone comes from reason. Besides, this nothingness is neither horrible nor peremptory. Have I not under my very eyes Nature's example of perpetual generation and regeneration? Nothing dies, my friend, nothing in this world is destroyed. Today a man, tomorrow a worm, the day after a fly, is that not aways existing? And why should you want me rewarded for virtues I am not worthy of, or punished for crimes I had no control over? Can you reconcile the goodness of your supposed God with this creed; can He have wanted to create me to give Himself the pleasure of punishing me, and that only as a result of a choice over which I have no control?

PRIEST: You have.

DYING MAN: Yes, according to your prejudices; but reason destroys these, and the creed of man's free will was only invented to forge that of grace, so propitious to your fantasies. What man is there in the world who, seeing the scaffold side by side with the crime, would commit if he were free not to commit it? We are swept along by an irresistible force, and are never for a moment masters enough to resolve anything other than the way our inclinations lie. There is not a single virtue that is not needed by Nature and, conversely, not a single crime that is not necessary to her. In the perfect equilibrium in which she keeps one and the other lies all her art; and can we be held guilty for the side to which she throws us? No more so than the wasp is that darts its sting into your skin.

PRIEST: So even the very greatest of all crimes should not inspire any terror in us.

DYING MAN: That is not what I said. It is enough for the law to condemn and for the sword of justice to punish to fill us with aversion or terror. But the moment we are so wretchedly committed, we must know what course to take and not abandon ourselves to barren remorse, for its action is useless since it cannot preserve us from it, void because it does not make amends for it; how absurd it is then to abandon ourselves to it; how much more absurd to fear being punished for crimes in another world, if we are so happy as to have escaped punishment in this one. Far be it from me to encourage crime on that score, for we must certainly avoid it as much as possible; but it must be avoided reasonably, and not by false fears that lead to nothing and whose effect is destroyed in a soul of any strength. Reason – yes, my friend, reason alone must tell us that injuring our brothers can never make us happy, and our heart alone must tell us that contributing to their joy is the greatest happiness Nature can give us on this earth. The whole of human morality is contained in this one saying: *make others as happy as you would wish to be yourself*, and

67

do them no more ill than you would wish to receive. There, my friend, there are the only principles we should follow; and there is no need for a religion or a god to relish them and admit them – there need only be a sound heart. Predicant, I feel I am weakening; leave your prejudices, be a man, be human, fearless and without expectation, leave your gods and your religions; they are only good for putting swords into men's hands, and the very name of these horrors has shed more blood on earth than all other wars and scourges together. Renounce the idea of another world; there is not one. But do not renounce the pleasure of being happy and causing happiness in this world. That is the only way Nature has to offer you of doubling or lengthening your life. My friend, sensual pleasure was always the dearest of my blessings; all my life I have been a votary and have wanted to end it in her arms. My end is near. In the next room are six women, more beautiful than the dawn. I have kept them for this moment. Be firm; try to forget on their breasts the empty sophisms of superstition and all the bloody errors of hypocrisy.

NOTE

The dying man rang, the women came in. and in their arms, the predicant became a man corrupted by Nature for not knowing how to explain what corrupted Nature is.

Preface to
CONTES ET FABLIAUX

[This preface, intended for a set of short stories to be called *Contes et Fabliaux du XVIIIe siècle par un troubadour provençal*, was drafted in the Bastille between 1787 and 1788, but was never published. Part of it was redrafted for publication as Preface to *Les Crimes de l'Amour* in 1800.]

NOTICE

The obligation under which every writer lies to conform to the tone of his century has, so to speak, imposed an *obligation* to make the serious tales in this collection extraordinarily heavy, and those that interlard them, for the sake of relaxation and to unknit the reader's brow, perhaps a shade too unrestrained. Everything deteriorates as it grows old; the refined and sensitive novels of Madame de La Fayette amused a public in Louis XIV's day, which, still steeped in chivalrous gallantry, and freshly come from its romances of the Round Table, would read with no repugnance the adventures of a heroine who made her lover sigh through nine volumes, and ended by a grand marriage in the tenth. In those days there were few books; there was time to turn pale over these insipidities; and in point of fact, it is not long since people made love to their fair ones just as these novels taught them to do.

The epicureanism of a Ninon de l'Enclos, of a Marion de Lorme, a Marquis de Sevigné, a La Fare, a Chaulieu, a Saint-Évremond, of all that engaging society which, derived from the languor of the god of Cythera, began to think what Fontenelle has subsequently expressed, that there was nothing good *in love but the physical*, somewhat changed the tone of the novel. Marivaux and Crébillion, who came after, and who felt that such languors would not amuse a century corrupted by the Regent, wrapped their immoralities and cynicism in a light, flowery, and sometimes even philosophical style. Perhaps it would have been as well to stop there; but the mind is to the *littérateur* what the stomach is to the gourmand. One and the other are satisfied by simple dishes at first, then by slow degrees they must be bettered by all the spices of the Orient.

Prévost appeared, and created, if we dare say so, the true genre of the novel. He alone knew the art of holding the interest for a length of time by a multitude of adventures that were always piquant, and that never let the reader's mind flag. They forced him into a necessary tension, the unfailing cradle of the most assured interest. He put masterpieces of the English novel into our language, and from the school of Fielding and Richardson he taught us that the reader is not always interested in virtue, that doubtless it is very fine and must be made to triumph as much as possible, but that this rule, which is not Nature's, but only what we would wish men to be subject to, is not in the least essential to the novel, and is not even that which conduces to interest. For when virtue triumphs, things being what they must be, my tears dry naturally; but if after the rudest trials, virtue comes, on the other hand, to succumb to the tireless efforts of vice, our hearts are torn and nothing is of avail, and the author's success is assured for having taken us to the utmost limits of interest. If after twelve or fifteen volumes, Richardson had finished virtuously by converting Lovelace, and had Clarissa peacefully married him, would we shed precious tears in spite of ourselves over this novel? Therefore it is

Nature that must be seized upon when working in this genre, and not morality; for however fine morality may be, it is only the work of man, and the novel must be a picture of Nature.

However that may be, it is certain that, after the novelists of the beginning and middle of this century, either one had to write like them to please, or one had to seek in Nature stronger hues that had escaped them. There was no necessity to retain the *soft vows* of Crébillon, but a need for broad sketching in, as in the author [Marivaux] of *Marianne*, and subtle variations, as in Prévost.

As for *La Nouvelle Héloïse*, it must be put out of sight; it is a kind of unique masterpiece that will never be equaled, and of which all copies are detestable. Today, unfortunately, people are not sufficiently convinced of this creed, which is why we get a flood of imbecilities aped from the *Héloïse*, of which it has become impossible to read a page because the tasteless, mindless authors of these platitudes have idiotically believed it was sufficient to mix yearnings with two or three strongish features to be as perfect as their original. They did not see that it was not this that was needed to create a second *Héloïse*, they did not feel that the indispensable thing was a soul of fire like Rousseau's and as philosophic a mind: two things that Nature does not bring off in one and the same century.

It must be confessed that in the tales we offer here the impetuosity we have allowed ourselves is not always in harmony with the wholesome, boring morality of Monsieur d'Arnaud's frigid tales. Yet, if we have not always been excessively virtuous, at least we have always been true, and Nature is more often twisted than straight. Her deviations had to be followed, and that we have done. And who, in a genre like this, could credit himself with bringing out virtue if he had not strongly accented the surrounding features of vice? The Marquise de Teleme (in the tale of that name) would be just as interesting even if the merchant who deceives her were not an abominable man; would Monrevel draw tears so sweet to shed if the Countess de Sancerre were not a villain? What would Laurence be, simply persecuted by a rival of Antonio, if this rival were not both his father-in-law and a lecherous monster? Etc.

We say: as tastes cloy, as minds grow corrupt, as people grow tired of tales, novels, and comedies, stronger things must of necessity be put before them, if one wants to succeed. In several of these tales we have used an absolutely new means, which the pious will unfortunately take exception to, whatever good effects we may reasonably expect. The basis of nearly all tales and nearly all novels is a young woman, loved by a man who is akin to her, and crossed in her love by a rival whom she dislikes. If this rival triumphs, the heroine, they say, is extremely unfortunate; but in the present century (this must always be the starting point) with the present depraved state of morals, would the familiar romantic castastrophe really plunge a girl into the last excesses of misery? Considering the prevailing case with which a young woman consoles herself for a displeasing husband, can she complain today of being handed over to a spouse of this kind . . . ?

This, then, is what has decided us to add an extra touch, more than age and ugliness, to the rival who crosses the heroine's loves. We have given him a tinge of vice or of libertinism to alarm truly the girls he tries to seduce, and finding themselves in this way menaced by a fate infinitely more deadly than those that have frightened up to now, these young persons inevitably acquire a completely different interest. An ugly old man who masters a girl certainly makes the creature pitiable, but this ill is less real when washing, dressing, and a young lover can at once dispel the memory of these slight setbacks. If, on the other hand, either the rival lover, or the husband already taken, by an inconceivable series of depravities, of scandalous conduct, cruel whims, and shameful ones, too, threatens the young and tender victim that he pursues with a never-ending sequence of moral and physical calamities, would you not tremble to see him triumph? Cold-blooded people will be scandalized at these deviations, however little they may be used these days; but what a very different pleasure for warm-blooded, vigorous readers, to whom all that is interesting is pleasing, and who in their knowledge of the wrongs of Nature love to follow her most tortuous paths – to both study and know man, and to groan at the misfortunes into which he inevitably falls, if by virtuous principles he does not break the influence of capricious Nature on his weak pusillanimous soul.

No doubt it was necessary to hide such monstrosities of man's intemperance in those artless and virtuous ages when the very word love was scarcely spoken; but with morals so perverse, one has been able to lift a small corner of the veil and to say to man: this is what you have become, *mend your ways for you are repulsive.*

And in the most distant centuries, even in those of chivalry, were these depravations unknown that we have occasionally used and that were forbidden in the pictures of man? Boccaccio, Bandello, the Duchess d'Alençon, our troubadours: did they not put them to use, and is it not frequently on this score that they have aroused interest? There are other passions than jealousy, revenge, and ambition to put into play to interest the reader; other springs

71

can be moved in the heart of man. To move them successfully, our new genre has used reticence; there is nothing to be feared on this side, and the most respectable of women can read us without a change of expression.

Yet, there is some bawdiness in our merry tales, we do confess; but as a great wit said: *In tales it is permissible to make merry and to take liberties that would be out of place in a serious work.*

Great men have not blushed to use this genre. Sisenna, the Roman praetor and member of the Cornelii, translated licentious Milesian fables; Petronius, consul, diverted us with the debaucheries of Nero. What censor is there so severe that he would not smile at the guileless ingenuity of the Scholar of Pergamus, whom St. Louis, nevertheless, would have burnt? As we know, they accused Boccaccio of being an *atheist* for having written those charming novelettes . . . but we are no longer under the sway of monks, and the word *atheist* is no longer abuse. They censured him further: *Chi potesse contare* (said Boniface Vanozzi) *quante putane ha fatto il decamerone rimmarebbe stupido et senza senzo* – another critic we are not afraid of. *Adhesso*, we might say, *le putane sono fatte non che piu periculoso*. So good women will shed tears on reading our tragic tales, and they will honor with a smile those that seem a little licentious; and in the certainty that it is pleasantry, they will neither take alarm nor be corrupted by them. *Ma per le putane* they shall not make one step more in the infamous career they are embarked upon; in these gay tales we have done virtue no harm, and rest assured, we have not encouraged vice. There remain the monks . . . but they are not listened to . . . the pious, but there will be egoism, and they won't dare; there remain, lastly, those little fleeting authors and those ill-formed fabricators of thirty volumes a year, compilers or absurd plagiarists who bring disgrace upon literature, and who, furious at seeing in these tales that the language they mangle every day is fairly correctly spoken and that there are other ways of being interested in it than by their hackneyed petty tricks, will perhaps mob against us as much as they can. But we despise them, being too far above them to see them; we cannot even hear their yapping, still less reply to it. To speak or busy ourselves with them would be to draw them out of the bog where their pitiable writings damn them eternally.

For the rest, all these tales are new. None is embroidered on well-known stock; only one, 'The Enchanted Tower,' has some historical foundation, and a slight strain of another, 'The Marquise de Teleme,' is to be found in Madame Dunoyer. It will be seen from the sincerity of our confessions that we are far from taxing the reader's patience by compilations or thefts; in this genre, one must be new, or leave it alone. . .

We should be much more certain of current praise if we had copied Richardson or Rousseau, but we are sorry to say our tales are our own. . . .

From
EUGENIE DE FRANVAL

1

When Eugénie reached the age of seven, Franval took her to his wife. This affectionate parent, who had not seen her own child since she brought it into the world, was unable to caress her enough; she held her two hours tightly to her bosom and covered her with kisses and tears. She wanted to know what little talents she had; but Eugénie had only those of reading fluently, enjoying the most vigorous health, an being as beautiful as an angel. Madame de Franval's despair was renewed when she realized that it was only too true that her daughter was ignorant of even the first principles of religion.

'What, sir,' she said to her husband, 'are you bringing her up for in this world? Have you not stopped to consider that she may not live in it more than a moment? Like us, she will plunge into fatal eternity, if you deprive her of something that will allow her to enjoy a happy fate at the feet of the Being to whom she owes her life.'

'Madame,' replied Franval, 'if Eugénie knows nothing, if these maxims have been carefully kept from her, she cannot be unhappy. For if they are true, the Supreme Being is too just to punish her for her ignorance, and if they are false, what need is there to talk to her of them? As for other cares of her education, I beg you to trust me; as from today I am her teacher, and I declare that in a few years, your daughter will surpass every child of her own age.'

Madame de Franval wanted to stand her ground, calling on the eloquence of the heart to support that of reason, and a few tears appeared to aid her. But Franval, who was not softened by them, did not even seem to notice. He had Eugénie taken away, saying to his wife that if she had it in her mind to thwart in any way whatsoever the education he aspired to give his daughter, or if she suggested principles other than those he was going to nourish her on, she would deprive herself of the pleasure of seeing her, for he would place his daughter in one of his châteaux. Madame de Franval yielded and was silent. She implored her husband not to separate her from so dear a possession, and tearfully promised to disturb no single part of the eduction that was being planned.

From now on, Mademoiselle de Franval was boarded in a very fine apartment next to her father's, with a most intelligent governess, an undergoverness, a chambermaid, and two girls of her own age to play with. She had writing masters and tutors in drawing, poetry, natural history, elocution, geography, astronomy, anatomy, Greek, English, German, Italian, fencing, dancing, riding, and music. Every day Eugénie rose at seven, whatever the time of year. Running out into the garden, she went to eat a large portion of rye loaf, which was her entire breakfast. She returned at eight, and spent a few moments in her father's room, while he frolicked with her or taught her parlor games. She got ready for her exercises until nine when the first master arrived; she received five before two o'clock. Dinner was served apart with her two playmates and the first governess; it consisted of vegetables, fish, pastries, and fruit – never of any meat, soup, wine, liqueurs, or coffee. From three to four, Eugénie went back to the garden to play for an hour with her young friends; and they practiced tennis, playing at ball, skittles, and kites, or running marked distances. They made themselves comfortable according to the season; here there was no constricting the waist; they were never imprisoned in those ridiculous whalebones, as dangerous to the stomach as to the chest, and which, by hindering a young person's breathing inevitably attack the lungs. From four to six, Mademoiselle de Franval received new teachers, and as all were unable to appear the same day, more came the day after. Three times a week, Eugénie went to the theater with her father, in a little railed box hired for her by the year. At nine she returned to supper. Only vegetables and fruit were served. Four times a week, from ten to eleven, Eugénie played with the women, read a few novels, and then went straight to bed. The other three days, when Franval was not supping out, she went alone to her father's apartment, and this time was employed in what Franval called 'her lectures.' There he instilled into his daughter his maxims on morality and religion; on the one hand, he presented her with what certain men thought on these matters, and on the other, he established what he himself believed.

With great spirit, wide knowledge, a keen mind, and passions already aflame, the progress of Eugénie's soul under such methods may be readily believed; but as the outrageous Franval was not content with improving the mind, his lectures rarely came to an end without exciting the heart, and this horrid man had so exactly hit on the means of pleasing his daughter, he instigated her with such art, he made himself so essential to her education and her pleasures, he so enthusiastically whirled ahead of all that she might like, that Eugénie, even surrounded by the most brilliant company, found nothing so likable as her father. Even before she had explained his conduct, the innocent and yielding creature had gathered in her young heart all the feelings of friendship, gratitude, and tenderness that cannot fail to lead to burning love, and for him. In society she saw only Franval; he alone was distinct; and she fought against the very idea of anything that could have separated her from him. She would have lavished on him, not her honor, not her charms, for all these sacrifices would have seemed too slight for the tender object of her idolatry, but her blood, her very life, if this dear companion of her soul had asked it.

The impulse of Mademoiselle de Franval's heart was by no means the same toward her respectable and unfortunate mother. The father, by shrewdly informing his daughter that Madame de Franval, being his wife, demanded attentions from him that often prevented his doing all for his dear Eugénie that his heart dictated, had found the secret of putting far more of hatred and jealousy in this young person's soul than the tender and considerate feelings that should have awakened there for such a mother.

'My friend, my brother,' Eugenie would say sometimes to Franval, who would have his daughter use no other expressions with him, 'this woman you call yours, this creature who, as you say, brought me into the world, is indeed very demanding, since by wanting you always by her side she is depriving me of the happiness of spending my life with you. I see very well that you prefer her to your Eugénie. I, I shall never love what takes your heart away from me.'

'My dear,' replied Franval, 'no, no being in the whole universe shall gain as powerful a right as yours. The ties between this woman and your best friend are the fruits of custom and social convention, and since I view them philosophically, they shall never sway those that bind us. . . . You will always be my favorite, Eugénie; you shall be the angel, the light of my days, the home of my soul, and the power behind my existence.'

'Oh, how tender your words are!' replied Eugénie. 'Tell me often, my friend. . . . If only you knew how these words of love charm me!'

And taking Franval's hand she placed it on her heart. . . . 'Here, I feel them all here,' she went on.

'How your soft caresses reassure me,' replied Franval, taking her into his arms . . . and so the treacherous man, with no trace of remorse, brought about the seduction of this unhappy girl.

2

In the meantime Eugénie had reached her fourteenth year, and here was the age at which Franval wanted to consummate his crime. Tremble! . . . For he did.

The day she came to this age, or rather when this course of time was run, as both of them were in the country, without relations or any embarrassments, the Count, after first decking his daughter that day like virgins that in ancient times were dedicated in the temple of Venus, had her appear in a luxurious drawing-room, towards ten o'clock in the morning. The lighting was softened by gauze, and the furniture was strewn with flowers. A throne of roses stood out in the center. Franval led his daughter to it.

'Eugénie,' he said, seating himself, 'today – be the queen of my heart, and let me adore you on bended knees.'

'You, my brother, adore me, when it is I who owe you everything, when you made me, formed me . . . oh, rather let me fall at your feet, it is my only place, the only one I aspire to with you.'

'O my dear Eugénie,' said the Count, drawing near her on these flowered seats that were to assist his triumph, 'if you truly owe me something, if the feelings you show me are as sincere as you say, do you know the way to convince me?'

'And what is it, my brother, tell me quickly, that I may grasp it with all my heart?'

'Eugénie, all those charms Nature has lavished upon you, all the attractions she has beautified you with, you must sacrifice to me at once.'

'But why are you asking me? Are you not the master of all; doesn't what you made belong to you; can another enjoy your handiwork?'

'But you know the prejudices men have.'

'You have never hidden them from me.'

'I do not wish to transgress them without your consent.'

'Do you not despise them as I do?'

'Yes, but I do not wish to be your tyrant, even less so your seducer. The blessings I ask for I want only out of love. You know the world, and I have never concealed its attractions from you, never kept men from your eyes; not to let you see anything but me would have been a deceit unworthy of me. If there is a being in the world you prefer to me, name him at once, and I will go to the ends of the earth to find him and fetch him at once into your arms. In a word, it is your happiness, my angel, that I want, yours much more than mine. These pleasures, then, that you can give me would be nothing to me, if they were not the reward of your love. Decide then, Eugénie; you are near to being immolated, as you must be; but name the sacrificer yourself. I renounce the pleasures that title secures me if they do not come from your soul and are unworthy of your heart. If it is not me you prefer, at least by bringing you someone you can cherish I shall have deserved your affection. If I have been unable to capture your heart, I shall be Eugénie's friend, having failed to be her lover.'

'You shall be all, my brother, you shall be all,' Eugénie said, burning with love and desire. 'To whom would you have me sacrifice myself, if not to the only one I adore. What being in the world can be more worthy than you of the the feeble charms you desire . . . and that your feverish hands search for so fervently already. Can you not see by the fire that consumes me that I am as eager as you to know the pleasure you talk of? Ah, take me, dear brother, best of friends, make your Eugénie your victim; sacrificed by your dear hands, she will ever be exultant!'

Our passionate Franval, who, conforming to the character we know him to have, had only paraded such tact the more shrewdly to seduce, soon took advantage of his daughter's credulity; and once all obstacles were set aside, he made his wicked conquest as much by the principles he had nourished in this impressionable soul as by the art he used to capture it at this late moment. He became with impunity the destroyer of a virginity that both Nature and his capacity had confided to him to defend. Several days went by in mutual ecstasy. Eugénie was of an age to know the pleasures of love and, encouraged by his method, applied herself unreservedly; and Franval taught her all the secrets, showed her every way. As his homage grew, his captive was more closely bound; she would have him pay respects in a thousand temples at once; she charged her friend's imagination with not being sufficiently perverse; it seemed to her that he concealed something; she blamed her age and her ingenuousness that perhaps did not make her seductive enough. If she wished to be more knowledgeable, it was only so that no means of exciting her lover should remain unknown to her.

They returned to Paris. But the criminal pleasures this perverse man had reveled in had been so exquisite a flattery to his moral and physical talents that the unfaithfulness that usually broke up all his other intrigues could not sever the knots of this one. He fell desperately in love, and from that dangerous passion the inevitable result was his most heartless neglect of his wife . . .

3

'Well, Eugénie,' Franval said to his daughter that evening, 'as you can see, they want to make us part. Shall they succeed, my child? Will they manage to break the sweetest bonds of my life?

'Never, never! Oh, my dearest friend, do not fear. These bonds you delight in are as precious to me as to you. You did not deceive me; I see by making them how far they outrage our customs; and being so little afraid of transgressing habits that vary from clime to clime and can have nothing sacred about them, I wanted these bonds; I have forged them without any regrets. Do not fear that I will break them.'

'Alas, who knows? Colunce is younger than I am. He has everything to captivate you; pay no heed, Eugénie, to the last throes of a madness that doubtless blinds you. Age and the light of reason, by dispelling the glamor, will soon cause regrets which you will lay in my heart, and I shall never forgive myself for being their begetter!'

'No,' Eugénie replied firmly, 'no, I have decided to love you alone. I should think myself the unhappiest of women if I had to take a husband. . . .

'I,' she continued warmly, 'I, to be joined to a stranger who, not having like you twin reasons for loving me, would make his desires the very limit of his feelings . . . abandoned, despised by him, what would become of me afterwards? Should I be prude, saint, or whore? No, no – I would rather be your mistress, my friend, a hundred times so than be reduced to playing one of these infamous roles in society. . . .

'But what is the cause of all this?' she went on bitterly. 'Do you know it? Do you know her? Your wife? She, only she, and her implacable jealousy; there, without doubt, is the true cause of the misfortunes that threaten us. Oh, but I do not blame her; it is all too easy and understandable when it is a matter of keeping you. What would I not do in her place, if someone wanted to steal your heart?'

Franval was amazingly moved, and embraced his daughter a thousand times. She, further encouraged by these criminal caresses and fostering her evil soul with even more energy, went so far as to suggest to her father, with unforgivable effrontery, that the only way of being less observed was to procure a lover for her mother.

This plan amused Franval; but being even more wicked than his daughter, and wishing to prepare this young heart imperceptibly for all the brands of hatred against his wife that he wished to impress on it, he replied that this seemed too lenient a revenge, and that there were many other means of making a woman unhappy when she put her husband on his mettle.

4

Madame de Franval bribed one of Eugénie's women; a pension, good prospects, the semblance of a worthy act, all this determined the creature, and she promised, as from the following night, to put Madame de Franval in the way of confirming her misfortunes.

The moment came. The wretched mother was shown into a room next to the apartment where her falsehearted husband outraged all heaven and his bonds of marriage every night. Eugénie was with her father; several candles were still alight in a corner to illuminate the crime . . . the altar was ready, and the victim took her place . . . the sacrificer followed. . . . Madame de Franval . . . broke the doors that held her back and threw herself into the room; there, falling tearfully on her knees at the feet of the incestuous pair. . . .

'You,' she cried at Franval, 'the despair of my life, from whom I have not deserved such treatment; you whom I still worship despite the wrongs I receive from you, witness my tears, and do not spurn me. . . .'

From
ALINE ET VALCOUR

We had been walking for about two hours. The sun began to shine, and it was a pleasure to see the first rays gild the waving heads of a magnificent cornfield, the edge of which we were following. Suddenly we saw two women in a corner of this field, in tears, and raising their hands to heaven.

'Quick, my friends,' cried Brigandos, 'perhaps this is an occasion for doing good – we indulge in evil so often.'

We instantly ran up to these women, shouting to them not to be afraid and to tell us the cause of their grief.

They were too perturbed to reply, and while still weeping, they pointed to three men on horseback, galloping full tilt through this rich harvest, snapping the stalks, making the ears fly, and destroying in a minute a measure of the hope and work of an entire family. . . .

'Sir knight,' one of these women said at last to our leader, her voice broken with sobs, 'this is my father's field, and there are fifteen of us who live on its produce the whole year round. . . The climate has been in our favor this season, and the good old man wanted to put a small sum to one side to marry my young sister here, but my poor dear father will not have that comfort. . . . These men you see galloping through our property have been doing this same thing for three days. It's the parish priest, sir, with his curate and sexton. They've done us more harm than four storms in one summer.'

'But why?' asked Brigandos.

'One of his parishioners,' the woman went on, 'whose house you can see down there, has been very ill for several days. He sent for the pastor, and he, to come to the aid of the dying man as quickly as possible, as he expects a considerable legacy, crosses our field, as you see, instead of taking the highway. He doesn't want his penitent to die without his ministration, and he claims that going as the crow flies saves him three-quarters of an hour. The day before yesterday he went there to admonish him, yesterday for the holy oil, and today I don't know why, but he is ruining us, sir, ruining us.'

And the two unhappy women began to shed their tears again. In the meantime the priest cleaved the air, and as he was coming in our direction, he was scarcely more than thirty paces away when Brigandos in his fury cried at him in a voice of thunder to stop instantly, or he would be dead. But the holy man went galloping on and promptly produced from the fob of his breeches a small tin box; the curate uncovered his head and recited a few paternosters, the sexton made the air resound with a hand bell, and all three, without stopping, continued to harvest the field.

'By Lucifer's beard,' cried Brigandos, who was getting hotheaded in his wrath, 'stop, you greybeards, or I'll bury you under the corn you're breaking!'

'Infidel,' the priest cried at him, 'surely you see that I am carrying God?'

'If you bore the Devil,' our leader rejoined, 'you would get no further, or I'd disembowel you.'

And as our men all advanced on these three riders together, they had to come to a halt. The two women were still there, not knowing what Brigandos would do.

'Sir,' the Bohemian said, briskly unseating the priest, 'where did you learn that you had to destroy a sound man's heritage in order to bear God to a sick one? Are there no roads in the district? Why don't you use 'em?'

'Should I let a man go to Hell out of consideration for a few grains of corn?'

'Understand, stupid knave,' cried Brigandos, grasping the pastor's neck sharply, 'that the humblest blade of corn that Nature grants for the upkeep of these unfortunates is a hundred times more worthy and valuable than all the doughy idols in your disgusting breeches; and remember that it is with this corn that the gods you carry are made, and that if you destroy the raw material, their holy species will be unable to reproduce.'

'Arrant blasphemer!'

'Please, no compliments, I am not obstructing your duties to hear myself praised by you, but to have you make good instantly the wrongs you have been doing to these good people for three days See them weeping at your crimes, and dare to say that you are God's servant after that.'

'I, make good?'

'Yes, and by all devildom, you must.'

'How then?'

'By you three disbursing here the sum of one hundred piastres, at which I value approximately the damage you have done to these peasants.'

'A hundred piastres? They could not be found in the whole parish.'

'We will verify that,' said our captain, making a sign to his men to do as he did.

Upon this he leaped on the pontifical breeches, and first found the holy box: 'Oh for this gem,' he said, hurling it forty feet over his head, 'I wouldn't give a damn.'

And completely unbreeching the pastor, he eventually uncovered an old leather purse.

Then turning to his comrades, while the priest restored his unveiled modesty in the background: 'Well, lads,' he said, 'see if your hunting has been as good as mine. Add it up. . . . '

The three purses were emptied, and yielded a total of ten piastres more than our leader's assessment.

'Come here, my good women,' our captain went on, calling the plaintiffs . . . 'Here, take what the Bohemian tribunal awards you as damages for what has been done to you.'

'Oh, sir, sir,' cried these women, bathing their Solomon's hands with tears. . . . 'Alas, we are indeed happy, but this man of God you have just sentenced is wicked, and you will not have gone very far before he will return to take back what you have so justly awarded us.'

'Take it back? My band will not leave the neighborhood of this this farm for two weeks,' Brigandos said to the priest, 'and, rogue, if so foul a deed enters your head, I will make you eat your balls on a skewer. . . . Here, take the rest of your money, I am not like officers of the law. . . . Pick up your God. . . . Get on your beast . . , stop thinking that what you were doing was a good thing that could be bought at the price of the evil your stupidity dared permit you; the good was only imaginary, the ravages incontestible. Remember, my friend, that what is called good, is only the useful, and that the useful is never fulfilled so long as it costs poverty a tear.'

The priest was abashed, having perhaps never said anything so philosophical from the pulpit, and ran off at once to find his box. But while the case was being judged, an unusual thing happened; one of our women, pressed by a desire of some consequence, had hidden herself in the corn with the intention of going about it with as much satisfaction as modesty. Either by chance, or by temptation, the wretched box was there, and it had fallen open; its inside received her superfluity, and it was in this sorry state of increase that the reliquary greeted the pastor. Too abashed to dare complain, he contented himself with crossing himself three times, put his gods and their seasoning in his pocket, then, straddling his brood mare, he took leave of our chief, who swore that if he behaved, he would be friends nonetheless.

All went their various ways. The young peasant women were so entranced by their judge that they begged him to come and spend at least two days in their home with his band.

From

LES INFORTUNES DE LA VERTU

'My child, the harshness of the rich justifies the knavery of the poor. Let their purse come open to our needs, let humanity reign in their hearts, and then perhaps virtue will reside in ours. But so long as our misfortune, our patience under it, our trust and our bondage serve merely to augment our irons, then our crimes become their doing, and we should be foolish indeed to spurn such crimes in order to lessen a little the yoke they place on us. Nature, Sophie, made us all equal at birth; if Fate is pleased to upset the first project of the general laws of Nature, it is up to us to correct her caprices, and to use our cunning to set right the encroachment of the strongest. How I love to hear them, these rich people, these judges, these magistrates – how I love to hear them preaching virtue at us; indeed, it is very difficult to keep from stealing when one has three times more than enough to live by, very difficult not to conceive murder when surrounded only by sycophants or obedient slaves. Enormously difficult, in truth, to be temperate and sober when pleasure intoxicates and the most succulent dishes are all around. How hard for them to be frank, when no occasion ever arises in which it is to their interest to lie! But we, Sophie, we whom this barbarous providence you have been so foolish as to make your idol has condemned to crawl upon the earth like the serpent in the grass, we who are eyed only with disdain, because we are poor, we, in short, who find only gall and thorns on the whole surface of the world, you would have us deny ourselves crime, when crime alone can open the door of life to us, maintain us, keep us alive, or prevent us from losing our lives; you, while the class that is our master keeps all fortune's favors to itself, you would have us, perpetually submissive and humble as we are, own nothing but suffering, dejection, and pain, nothing but want and tears, mutilation and the scaffold. No, no, Sophie, no, either the providence you worship is made only for us to scorn, or those are not its intentions. . . . Know it better, Sophie, know it better, and realize that the moment it [Nature] places us in a situation where evil is our necessity, and at the same time allows us the opportunity of doing evil, it is becase this evil obeys her laws even as good does, and because one is as rewarding to her as the other. The state in which we are created is one of equality, and whoever upsets it is no more to blame than he who tries to re-establish it, for both act according to the impulses they receive, both follow them, averting their eyes and enjoying their acts.'

From the Introduction to
LES 120 JOURNEES DE SODOME

1

Such, dear reader, were the eight principal characters with whom we shall cause you to live. Now it is time to reveal to you the object of the strange pleasures that were projected.

True libertines agree that sensations received through hearing are those that gratify most and give the liveliest impressions; and so our four scoundrels, wishing pleasure to instill their hearts in as deep and predatory a way as possible, had conceived a tolerably strange plan to achieve it.

After surrounding themselves with everything that could best satisfy their other senses by lubricity, it was a question of having themselves, in this situation, told, categorically and in the greatest detail, all the different varieties of this debauch, all its adjuncts, in a word, all that debauchery names as the passions. The degree to which man diversifies them when his fancy is kindled surpasses imagination; if men differ excessively in all their other idiosyncrasies, all their other tastes, by so much the more do they in this case; and if one could capture and catalogue these wayward varieties, he would perhaps produce one of the finest works to be seen on manners, and possibly one of the most interesting. It was, then, a matter of first finding persons able to report on all these excesses, to analyze them, enlarge on them, go into detail, grade them, and through all this, insert the interest of a tale. This, in consequence, was resolved upon. After innumerable searches and enquiries, they found four women already past the prime of life, as indeed was necessary, experience being in this case the most essential thing, four women, as I was saying, who had spent their lives in the most excessive debauchery and who were now in fine frame to report exactly on all these pursuits. As they had been selected carefully for the gift of a certain eloquence and a turn of mind suitable to what was demanded of them, they were able to place, each one of them, in the experiences of their lives all the most extraordinary deviations of debauchery, and these in such an order that the first, for example, filled her tale of the events of her life with the hundred and fifty most elementary passions, the least far-fetched deviations, or the most ordinary; the second filled in a similar outline with an equal number of strange passions,

84

and with one man, or several men, and several women; equally, the third in her story had to introduce a hundred and fifty manias most criminal and outrageous to the law, nature, and religion, and since all these excesses lead to murder and since sexual murders are infinite in their variety, and the lecher's fired imagination assumes different punishments on as many occasions, the fourth was obliged to add to the happenings of her life a detailed account of a hundred and fifty of these various tortures. During all this our libertines, surrounded, as I have said, first with their women and then by other objects of every kind, listened, grew hotheaded, and finally extinguished either with these women or with these different objects, the fires these taletellers had kindled. There is, without any shadow of doubt, nothing more pleasurable than the inordinate way they went about it. . . .

As the four actresses in question play a fundamental role in this dissertation, we believe ourselves, if the reader will excuse us, further obliged to depict them; they will reminisce and they will perform – is it possible, after this, to leave them unknown? Let no one expect portraits of beauties, although without a doubt there were schemes to use these four creatures physically as well as morally. Nevertheless it was neither their attractions nor their age that were decisive, but simply their mind and experience, and in that direction it was impossible to be better provided.

Madame Duclos was the name of the woman instructed to relate the hundred and fifty simple passions. She was forty-eight years old, still tolerably fresh, with considerable remains of some beauty, extremely fine eyes, a very white skin, and one of the plumpest and most admirable backsides to be seen; a clean fresh mouth; a magnificent bosom, and dark, pretty hair; solidly built but tall, and with all the air and breeding of a whore of quality. As we shall see, she had spent her life in places where she was in a position to study what she was going to tell, and it was evident that she would set about it with wit, ease, and interest.

Madame Champville was a large woman of about fifty, slender, well built, a most sensual air about her figure and her look. A faithful disciple of Sappho, whose manner she had caught down to the least movement, the slightest gesture, and the briefest phrase; she had been ruined by keeping women, and if it had not been for this taste, to which, in the main, she had sacrificed all she earned in the world, she would have been comfortably well off. For a very long time she had been a public prostitute and for several years she had taken a turn at the profession of dresser, but she was hardened to a certain number of experienced and inveterate debauchees, all of a certain age, for she never received young persons; this prudent and lucrative conduct restored her fortunes somewhat. She had been fair-haired, but a discreeter shade was now tinting her head; her eyes retained their great beauty, were blue, and pleasing in expression. Her lips were attractive, still fresh, and perfectly unimpaired; *pas de gorge, le ventre bien, elle n'avait jamais fait d'envie, la motte un peu elevée et le clitoris saillant de plus de 3 pouces quand il etoit echaufé, en la chatouillant sur cette partie on etait bientot sur de la voir se pamer et surtout si le service lui etait rendu par une femme, son cul etait tres flasque et tres usé, entierrement mou et fletrie et tellement endurci par des habitudes libidineuses que son histore nous expliquera, qu'on pouvait y faire tout ce qu'on' voulait sans qu'elle le sentit. . . .*

La Martaine, a vast mama of fifty-two, blooming, healthy, and possessed of the largest and finest rump that could be, was in quite contrary case. *Une difformité de la nature, elle était barrée, l'ayant empechée de connaitre autre chose, elle s'etait livrée a cette espece de plaisir entrainé et par cette impossibilité de faire autre chose, et par de premieres habitudes, moyen en quoi elle s'en tenait a' cette lubricité dans laquelle on pretend qu'elle etait encor delicieuse, bravant tout, ne redoutant rien, les plus monstruex engins ne l'effraiyaient pas, les preferoit meme, et la suite de ces memoires nous l'offrira peut-etre combattant valeureusement encor sous les etendarts de Sodome comme le plus intrepide des bougres. Elle avait des traits assés gracieux, mais un air de langueur et de deperissement commençait a fletrir ses attraits, et sans son embonpoint qui la soutenait encor, elle eut pu deja passer pour tres usée.*

As for Madame Desgranges, she was vice and lust personified. Tall, thin, fifty-six years old, of ghastly and emaciated complexion, dull eyes, dead lips, she represented the image of crime about to perish for lack of strength. She had at one time been dark, and it was even said that she had had a fine body, but not much later it had become a mere skeleton that could only inspire disgust. *Son cul fletri, usé, marqué, dechiré ressemblait plutot a du papier marbré qu'a'de'la peau humaine et le trou en etiot tellement large et ridé que les plus gros engins, sans qu'elle le sentit pouvaient y penetrer a sec.* To crown her graces, this bountiful Cytherean athlete, wounded in several engagements, had one breast missing and three fingers severed; she limped, and was short of six teeth and an eye. . . . If her body was the image of ugliness, her soul was the resting place of all the vices and all the most unspeakable crimes; an incendiary, a parricide, incestuous, sodomitic Lesbian, murderess poisoner, guilty of rape, theft, abortions and sacrilege, it could be truthfully affirmed that there was no single crime in the world this villainous woman had not committed or caused to be committed. Her present occupation was pimping; she was one of society's accredited purveyors, and as she combined a deal of experience with a pleasant jargon, she had been chosen to fill the role of fourth actress, that is to say the one whose account should offer the utmost in horrors and abominations. Who could play this character better than a creature who had committed them all?

2

Now Durcet's château stood in the middle of that small, well-surrounded, well-defended plain. Even so a wall thirty feet high encircled it, and beyond this wall a deep, water-filled moat guarded an *enceinte* in the shape of a rising walk. Finally, a low, narrow rear entrance penetrated to a large inner courtyard, around which all the living quarters were built. These quarters, vast in the extreme and very well furnished according to the latest arrangements, afforded, on the first floor, a huge arcade. .... From here one entered an elegant dining-room, set about with cupboards in the form of towers which, leading to the kitchens, made easy a hot, prompt service that dispensed with the agency of a servant. From the dining-room, furnished with carpets, canopies, ottomans, excellent armchairs, and all that could make it as comfortable as possible, one passed to a drawing-room, plain and unaffected, but exceptionally warm, and with good furniture. This room led to a reception room, set apart for the narrators' tales, being, so to speak, the battlefield for future fights; it was the seat of the lewd assemblies, and as it had been decorated accordingly, it merits a brief description on its own. It was semicircular in shape. In the curved part were four mirrored recesses, each fitted with a choice ottoman. By their construction, these four recesses faced square on the diameter that traversed the circle, and backing on the wall this diameter formed, was a throne raised to a height of four feet. This was for the narrator, and in a position that not only put her face to face with the four recesses intended for her audience, but which, as the circle was small, kept her within distance of it, so that not a word of her narrative should be lost. She was like an actress on the stage, and those in the recesses as it were in the amphitheater. Below the throne were tiers on which were to be found those destined to debauch, brought there to calm the senses that were exacerbated by the tales. Like the throne, these tiers were covered with a black velvet ornamented by gold fringes, and the recesses were done out in a similar and equally embellished material, but dark blue in color. At the base of each was a tiny door leading to an adjoining closet, and into this the subjects went from the tiers as they were wanted for the execution of these pleasures that were not to be performed in front of everybody. . . . These closets had sofas and all the furniture needed for every kind of pollution. On either side of the throne was a single column reaching to the ceiling. These two columns were intended to hold the subjects whom some misdemeanors had made liable to punishment; all the necessary instruments of punishment were hung up on the columns, an imposing sight that served to maintain that subordination so essential in arrangements of this kind, and of which is born almost all the charm of pleasure in the souls of the persecutors. This room led to a chamber at the extreme end of the apartment. This was a kind of boudoir, secret and completely soundproof, very heated, and dim even by daylight; it was set apart for close combat, and certain other pleasures. . . . To regain the other wing it was necessary to retrace one's steps; and once in the arcade – at the end of which a very fine chapel was to be seen – one re-entered the parallel wing, thus completing the tour of the inner courtyard. Here there was a magnificent ante-chamber leading to four beautiful apartments, each with its boudoir and closet; splendid beds *à la Turque*, in three-colored damask, and with furniture to match, decorated these apartments; and their boudoirs offered everything the most sensual and ingenious lechery could desire. These four rooms. were for the four friends, and they were very well quartered there...

The second story afforded roughly the same number of apartments, but differently allocated. First, on one side, was a huge apartment embellished with eight recesses, each with a divan, and this apartment was that of the girls. To one side were two small chambers for the old women who cared for them; beyond, two attractive rooms for two of the narrators; turning back, another similar apartment with eight alcove recesses for the eight boys; and again, two chambers for the two chaperons who were to watch over them; and beyond that, two corresponding rooms for the two other narrators. Above this were eight cells, and these were the quarters of the eight seducers, destined to spend very little time in their own beds. On the ground floor were the kitchens, with six cells for the six beings allocated to that work. They were three famous women cooks (preferred to men for this arrangement, and rightly so, I believe) with three sturdy girls to help them; but none of this was to be part of the pleasures; nothing of it was meant for that; and if the self-imposed rules were broken, it is because there are no bounds to lechery and because the true way of enlarging and multiplying one's desires is to wish to impose limits on them. One of these three servants was to care for the large amount of livestock that had been brought; for apart from the four old women who worked inside, there were absolutely no servants other than the three cooks and their helps.

But depravation, cruelty, loathing, bestiality, all these passions, felt or foreseen, had given rise to another quarter that demands a sketch. . . . Below the steps of the altar in the tiny Christian temple we noted in the arcade, a gravestone lifted skillfully. A very narrow, precipitous corkscrew staircase was discovered; and it led into the bowels of the earth by three hundred steps, to a kind of vaulted dungeon, enclosed by three iron doors, and in which were to be found the most atrocious things imaginable by the cruelest art and the subtlest barbarism, as much to terrify as to lead to horrors. And what peace reigned there; how reassured might be the villain whom crime took there with his victim! He was on his own, he was out of France, in a secure land, in the heart of an uninhabited forest, in a retreat in that forest that only the birds of the air might reach – such were the measures taken – here he was in the bowels of the earth. Woe, and woe a hundredfold to the hapless creature who found himself in such a forsaken place at the mercy of a lawless, faithless villain, whose pastime was crime whose sole interest in it was his passions, and who knew no restraint but the imperious laws of his own treacherous pleasures. . . .

Finally, when all was ready and all in perfect order, and the retainers installed, the Duke, the Bishop, and Curval with their brides set out and . . . not without extreme hardships, at last reached the château on the evening of the 29th of October. Durcet, who went ahead, had the mountain bridge cut as soon as they were over it. This was not all; the Duke, after examining the place, decided that since all provisions were on the inside and there was no further need to go out, to forestall attacks from the outside (these were only slightly apprehended) and escapes from the inside (these were more so), it was imperative to wall up all doors leading in, and to shut themselves in the place as in a besieged citadel, leaving not the least opening either to enemy or deserter. This decision was carried out. The barricading was such that it was no longer possible to recognize where the gates had been. . . . Two days remained until the first of November, and these were devoted to resting the staff so that they might be fresh the moment debauchery began. The four friends worked out a code of laws, signed by the heads and made known to the staff as soon as drawn up. . . .

From
LA PHILOSOPHIE DANS LE BOUDOIR

1

[Part of *La Philosophie dans le Boudoir* (1795) consists of an interpolated pamphlet which Dolmancé reads aloud to enlighten Eugénie and Madame de Saint-Ange. It is entitled: *Frenchmen! A further effort is needed if you would be republicans!*, and it is a résumé of Sade's philosophical, moral, and political ideas. The following is from the second part, 'Les Moeurs.']

Frenchmen! You are too enlightened not to feel that a new government will necessitate a new way of living; it is impossible for the citizen of a free state to behave as the slave of a despotic monarch; these differences in interests, duties, and relationships in themselves determine an entirely different fashion of behavior in society; a mass of minor faults and social transgressions deemed essential under the rule of kings, who had to be more and more demanding as they needed the restraints that would make them lofty and unapproachable to their subjects – all these will become meaningless. Other crimes, known by the names of regicide and sacrilege, under a government that knows neither kings or religions, must equally wither away in a republican state. In granting freedom of belief and freedom of the press, realize, Citizens, that at one remove from that you must accord freedom of action; that, excepting those things that bear directly against the government, there remain an uncounted number of crimes no longer punishable, for in reality there are very few actions that are criminal in a society based on freedom and equality, and if we scrupulously judge and examine matters, there is nothing truly criminal but what the law itself forbids. For Nature teaches us both vice and virtue in our constitution, or, in yet more philosophical terms, by reason of Nature's need for both vice and virtue, her promptings would become a true guide to the precise determinations of what is good or bad. In order the better to develop my ideas upon such an essential subject, let us classify the various actions of man's life which up to now have been named criminal, and we will then measure them against the true duties of a republican.

First, those which his conscience and his credulity impose on him towards the Supreme Being;

Second, those which he must fulfill towards his fellow men;

Third, and finally, those which relate only to himself.

The assurance we should feel that no god has ever had a hand in our existence and that we are here because it could not be otherwise, inevitable creatures of Nature like plants and animals – this assurance without doubt quite demolishes, as one can see, the first group of duties, those which we falsely believe we have towards divinity; and with them disappear all the religious transgressions, all those known under the vague and intangible names of *impiety, sacrilege, blasphemy, atheism*, etc: the transgressions, in fact which Athens punished so unjustly in Alcibiades, and France in the unfortunate Labarre. If there is one thing in the world grotesque beyond others, it is to see men, with only their own circumscribed ideas of their god and what this god demands, wish nevertheless to determine the nature of what pleases or angers this ridiculous phantom of their imagination. I would not stop at allowing all the sects an equal liberty; I should like a man to be free to ridicule and scoff at anything; I should like men gathered in this temple or the other and invoking the eternal, each in his own fashion, to look like comedians in a theatre whom anyone is free to go and laugh at. If you do not look at religions in this light, they will regain the seriousness that makes them seem of consequence; soon they will start to defend their views, and then it will not be a question of disputing religions but of fighting for them;[1] equality, destroyed by the preference or protection accorded to one religion, will soon vanish from the government, and out of *theocracy* reborn will spring *aristocracy*.

I cannot say this too often: no more gods, Frenchmen, no more gods, unless you wish their mournful rule to plunge you once more into all the horrors of despotism! Only you, by ridiculing them, can destroy them; all the dangers they bring with them will revive at once if you allow them scope and importance. Do not dash down their idols in anger; crush them in play, and prejudice will die out of itself.

This suffices, I hope to prove that no law should be passed against religious crimes – for he who offends against a myth offends no one – and that it is the utmost frivolity to punish those who outrage or despise a sect which has no apparent superiority

[1] Every people claims to have the best religion and bases it upon an infinity of proofs which are not only at odds with each other but almost entirely contradictory. In our present profound ignorance of what might please God (supposing that there is one), the wise course is either to protect all equally or forbid all equally; now, forbid them is assuredly the wisest, since we have the moral certainty that all are farces equally indifferent to a god who does not exist.

over any other; that would perforce mean taking sides and would at once influence the balance of equality, which is the prime law of your new government.

Let us pass to the second class of the duties of man, those which connect him with his fellows; this class is the most extensive of all.

Christian morality, far too vague on the subject of man's relation to his fellows, proposes axims so full of sophistry that we cannot admit them; for if one wishes to erect principles one must take care not to base them on sophistries. This absurd morality tells us to love our neighbor as ourselves. Nothing indeed could be more sublime, if only falsity did not often have the appearance of beauty. There is no question of loving one's neighbor as oneself, for that is against all the laws of Nature, and Nature should be the sole guide of our life; it is only a question of loving our fellow men as brothers, as friends given to us by Nature and with whom we will be able to live far better in a republican state, when distances between us are abolished and ties made closer.

Let humanity, fraternity, benevolence so prescribe our mutual duties, and let each one individually fulfill them with the amount of energy with which Nature has endowed him, without blaming and above all without punishing the phlegmatic or the melancholy who do not feel the same delight as others in these tender bonds; for, let us agree, it would be a palpable absurdity to wish to prescribe universal laws; it would be like the ludicrous procedure of a general who dressed all his soldiers in uniforms of the same size; it is a fearful injustice to expect men of different temperament to bow to the same laws; what suits one man does not suit all.

I agree that one could not make as many laws as there are men; but the laws could be so mild, so few, that all men, whatever their character, might easily obey them. Again, I would insist that these few laws be of a kind that could easily adapt themselves to different characters; and their administrator should be prepared to strike more or less severely according to the individual in question. It has been proved that such and such a virtue is impossible to certain men just as such and such a medicine cannot agree with a certain constitution. Therefore, what a consummation of injustice would it be to use the law to punish a man incapable of obeying that law! Would it not be an inquity equal to forcing a blind man to distinguish colors?

From these first principles develops the necessity for making benevolent laws, and above all for abolishing forever the death penalty, for a law that strikes at a man's life is impracticable, unjust, inadmissible. It is not – as I shall state – that there are not numberless cases when, without outraging Nature (and that is what I shall prove), men are given entire liberty by this common mother to attempt the life of other men, but that it is not possible for the law to have the same privilege, for cold-blooded law by itself cannot be subject to the passions that legitimize in man the cruel action of murder; man receives sensations from Nature that may make that action pardonable, while the law, on the contrary, always in opposition to Nature and receiving nothing from her, cannot be permitted the same licence; not having the same motives, it cannot have the same rights. These are knowing and subtle distinctions that escape many people, for there are few people who reflect; but they will be accepted by the thinking men to whom they are addressed, and they will, I hope, influence the new code that is being prepared for us.

The second reason for which the death penalty should be abolished is that it has never restrained crime, for crime is committed every day at the very foot of the scaffold.

This penalty must be abolished, in a word, because there can be no worse logic than to execute one man for having killed another, since the obvious result of this procedure is that two men are now dead instead of one, and only rascals and imbeciles are familiar with such arithmetic.

In sum, there are only four major crimes against our fellows: *calumny*, *theft*, offences caused by *uncleanness* which have a harmful effect on others, and *murder*.

Are all these actions, which are considered capital offences under a monarchal government, equally serious in a republican state? That is what we shall examine by the torch of reason, for it is by this light alone that we can conduct our enquiry. Let no one tax me with being a dangerous innovator; let no one say that there is a danger in awakening remorse in the souls of criminals, as these writings may do, that the leniency of my moral system will increase the criminals' leanings to crime; I formally testify that I have none of these perverse opinions; I am revealing the ideas I have held since I attained the age of reason, ideas opposed by the infamous despotism of tyrants for centuries; so much the worse for those who could be corrupted by these noble thoughts, who can only grasp evil from philosophic ideas and would be corrupted by anything. Perhaps they would be poisoned even by reading Seneca or Charon! It is not to them that I speak; I speak to those who are capable of understanding me, and they will be able to read me without danger.

I confess with complete frankness that I have never believed calumny to be an evil, especially under a government like our own, where all men are more united, more approachable, and therefore have more need to know each other well. Two things may result: either the calumny falls upon a man who is in fact wicked, or it falls on a virtuous man. You will agree that in the first case it makes very little difference whether evil is spoken of a man already known to do wrong; perhaps the falsely imputed crime will bring to light the true ones and make his villainy known.

If, let us suppose, there is an unhealthy climate at Hanover, but which would only expose me to an attack of fever, should I bear a grudge against a man who told me, to prevent me from going, that I should die on arriving there? Undoubtedly not; for by frightening me with a great danger he has saved me from a small one.

Should the calumny fall, on the contrary, on a virtuous man, let him have no fear; let him reveal himself frankly, and all the venom of the calumniator will recoil upon himself. For such men, calumny is only a purifying test from which their virtue emerges even brighter. The sum of virtue in the republic can even profit by this; for this virtuous and sensitive man, annoyed at the injustice he has experienced, will attempt to live better still; he will wish to overcome this attack from which he had thought himself safe, and his good deeds will acquire an extra degree of effort. Thus, in the first case, the calumniator will have brought about good results by exaggerating the vices of the dangerous man; in the second, he will produce even better results by forcing virtue to dedicate itself entirely to us.

Now, I ask you in what respect the calumniator can seem to you dangerous, especially in a society where it is essential to expose the vicious and increase the efforts of the virtuous? Let us take care then to establish no penalties for calumniation; rather, let us consider it as a searchlight or as an incentive, and as useful as either. The legislator, whose ideas must be as lofty as his task, should never study the effect of a crime which strikes only at individuals; he must study its effect on the mass of people, and when he thus observes the results of calumniation I defy him to discover anything punishable; on the contrary, he would be a truly just and sincere man if he were to favor and reward it.

Theft is the second of the moral offences which we propose to scrutinize.

If we scan antiquity, we find that theft was permitted and rewarded in all the Greek republics; Sparta and Lacedaemon openly favoured it; other peoples regarded it as a wartime virtue; certainly it maintains courage, strength, skill, all the virtues, in fact, which are useful to a republican government and thus to our government. I might venture to ask without prejudice whether theft, which tends to redistribute wealth, is really a great evil in a society whose whole aim is equality? No, undoubtedly not; for as it encourages equality on the one hand, on the other it makes people more watchful over their property. There was once a nation which punished, not the thief, but he who was robbed, in order to teach him to guard his property. This brings us to more detailed considerations.

Far be it from me to attack or overthrow the oath on the respect of property which the nation has just taken; but may I be allowed a few words on the injustice of this oath? What is the spirit of a vow made by all the individuals of a nation? Is it not to maintain a complete equality among the citizens, to place them all equally under the law protecting all property? Now, I ask whether a law which commands the man possessing nothing to respect the man who has everything is indeed just? What are the essentials of the social contract? Does it not consist in giving up a small amount of freedom and property in order to preserve both of them?

These principles underlie all laws; they motivate the punishment of those who abuse their liberty; they authorize taxes. When a citizen is asked to pay taxes, he does not complain because he knows that what he gives is used to preserve what remains with him; but once again, why should the man with nothing associate himself with a pact that protects only the man who has everything? If you are committing a just act in respecting, by your agreement, the properties of the rich, are you not committing an injustice in forcing the man who respects it, and yet has nothing, to submit to your agreement? What interest can he have in your agreement? And why do you expect him to make a promise that benefits only the man who differs so much from him by reason of his riches? There certainly could be nothing more unjust; an agreement should have the same effect for all the parties who subscribe to it; a man who has no interest in maintaining it cannot really be bound by it, for then it is no longer the pact of a free people; it becomes the law of the strong against the weak, who would then be in constant revolt against it. This then is what has taken place in the agreement on the respect of property which the nation has just passed; it is the rich man who binds the poor man to it; it is the rich man who gains from the promise made so unwillingly by the poor man, which he sees as a promise extorted from him in his good faith, and under which he agrees to do something that could never in fact be done to him.

Now that you are convinced, as you must be, of this barbarous inequality, do not aggravate the injustice of it by punishing the poor man for daring to rob the rich: your unfair agreement gives him a stronger right than ever. By forcing him to perjure himself through this meaningless agreement, you legitimize all the crimes which his perjury will bring about; thus it is not for you to punish what you yourself have caused. I will say no more to make you realize the horrible cruelty of punishing thieves. Imitate the wise law of the nation I mentioned; punish the man negligent enough to let himself be robbed, but inflict no penalty on the robber; reflect that it was your agreement that authorized him to do this, and that in giving in to it he is only following the first and most sacred impulse of Nature, that of preserving one's own existence at the expense of others.

The crimes which we now come to examine, in this second class of man's duties to his fellows, consist of the actions performed by libertinism, the most noteworthy of which are *prostitution, incest, rape* and *sodomy*. We should have no doubt that everything which goes under the name of moral crime, that is to say all the actions of the types we have just mentioned, are quite indifferent to a government whose sole duty is to maintain by one means or another a state of affairs that guarantees its existence — that is the only morality of a republican government.

Now, since this is always opposed by the tyrants who surround the country, one could scarely imagine reasonably that its means of defending this state could be *moral means*: for it can only defend itself by war, and nothing is less moral than war.

Now, I should like to ask how it could be proved that in a state that is obliged to be *immoral*, the individuals should be *moral*? I go further; I say it is better that they should not be. The legislators of ancient Greece fully realized the important necessity of corrupting the limbs of the state so that their *moral dissolution* influenced the vital parts of the body and resulted in insurrection, which is indispensable to a society that is as perfectly happy as is a republican society, a condition which is bound to excite the hatred and jealousy of surrounding states. Insurrection, these wise legislators believed, is certainly not a *moral* state; and yet it must be the permanent state of a republic; it would therefore be as absurd as it would be dangerous to demand that men who had to maintain a perpetual *immoral* disturbance of the machinery of state should themselves be very *moral* beings, for the moral state is one of peace and tranquillity, while the *immoral* state is one of perpetual movement, equivalent to the necessary state of insurrection into which the republican must guide his government.

Let us go into more detail now, and begin by analyzing modesty, that pusillanimous impulse that is hostile to all impure affections. If it were Nature's intention that man should be modest, she certainly would not have had him born naked; an infinite number of peoples, less degraded by civilization than we, go naked and feel no shame at it; there is no doubt that the custom of clothing oneself is simply caused by the inclemency of the climate, and by the coquetry of women; women felt that they would soon lose the effects of desire if they anticipated it; . . . thus modesty, far from being a virtue, was no more than one of the first effects of corruption, than one of the first means of female coquetry.

Lycurgus and Solon, who well understood that the results of immodesty held the citizen in the *immoral* state essential to the laws of republican government, required young girls to show themselves nude in the theaters.[2] Rome imitated this example: they danced nude in the fete of Flora; the majority of pagan rites were celebrated thus; nudity even passed for virtue with some peoples. Be that as it may, lewd propensities arise from immodesty and the results of these propensities make up the so-called crimes that we are analyzing, and of them the first result is prostitution.

Now that we are freed of all that pack of religious errors that formerly held us captive, and now that we are closer to Nature by reason of having demolished a quantity of prejudices, be assured that if there be a crime, it is rather to resist the desires that Nature has inspired in us (as well as to combat them); and, persuaded that desire was a result of these propensities, [be assured] that, rather than extinguish this passion in us, it is better to arrange the means for satisfying it in peace. We must then attempt to establish order here and to guarantee the necessary security to the citizen with a need to approach the objects of his desire, free to vent on these objects all those passions prescribed in him, without ever being restrained by anything; because there is no passion in man that needs so total an extension of liberty as this. Various health establishments, vast and suitably furnished, and secure in all points, will be erected in the city; there, all sexes, all ages, all creatures possible will be offered to the caprices of the libertines who wish pleasure; and the most complete subordination will be the rule for the individuals offered; the lightest refusal will be punished immediately and arbitrarily by him who has met with it. I must explain this further – the regulation of republican mores;

---

[2] It has been said that the intention of these legislators, in dulling the passion that men experience for a nude woman, was to render more active that which men experience now and then for their own sex. These sages required to be shown that which they wished to breed disgust for, and they hid that which they believed inspired the softest desires; in any case, did they work for any other end than that we have just described? They sensed, one realizes, the need for immorality in republican mores.

I have promised the same logic in everything, and I will keep my word.

If, as I have just said, there is no passion that so needs every possible extension of liberty as this one, there is also none that is so tyrannical; in this, man loves to command, to be obeyed, to surround himself with slaves constrained to satisfy him; now whenever you deny a man a secret means of expelling the deposit of tyranny that Nature has put into his heart, he will turn and vent it upon his surroundings; he will agitate against the government. If you wish to avoid this danger, allow a free scope to these tyrannical desires, which will torment a man in spite of himself; then, content at having wielded his petty sovereignty among the harem of Oriental servants and wives offered him by your money and organization, he will issue forth satisfied and with no desire to disturb a government that secures so willingly for him every object of his lusts; but should you, on the other hand, take different action and impose upon these objects of public lusts the ridiculous restraints formerly invented by ministerial tyranny and the lubricity of our Sardanapalus:[3] then each man will quickly become embittered against your government, jealous of the despotism that he sees you alone exercising, and will throw off the yoke with which you burden him and, tired of your fashion of ruling, will change it as he has just done.

Notice how the Greek legislators, thoroughly imbued with these ideas, treated debauchery in Lacedaemon and Athens; they intoxicated the citizen with it, far from forbidding it; no form of lechery was denied him; and Socrates, called by the oracle the wisest philosopher on earth, passed from the arms of Aspasia to those of Alcibiades and was not any less the glory of Greece. I will go further, and however opposed my ideas may seem to our present customs – since my object is to prove that we must hasten to change these customs if we wish to preserve our chosen government – I will try to convince you that prostitution for so-called decent women is no more dangerous than it is for men, and that we should not only involve them in the orgies in the brothels I would establish, but should even build some for them where their whims and the needs of their temperament, so differently passionate from ours, could be satisfied in the same way with all sexes.

By what right do you claim, first, that women should be exempted from the blind submission to men's whims that Nature ordains for them; and second, by what right do you claim to enslave them

---

[3] It is known that the infamous and rascally Sartine furnished a means of lust to Louis XV by having La Dubarry read to him three times a week the intimate details, embellished by himself, of all that happened in the low quarters of Paris. That particular libertinism of the French Nero cost the state three millions!

to continence, which is foreign to their nature and absolutely unnecessary to their honor?

I will treat these two questions separately.

It is certain that in a state of Nature women were born vulvovaginal, enjoying, that is to say, the advantages of other female animals, and like them belonging without exception to all males; such, doubtless, were the first laws of Nature and the only rules of the first societies made by men. *Self-seeking*, *egoism*, and *love* degraded these first simple and natural ideas; men believed they were adding to their wealth by taking a wife and her family inheritance; that is how the first two emotions I have mentioned came into being; yet more often men carried off their women and grew attached to them; that is how the other motive was born; and with it in every case went injustice.

Never can an act of possession be carried out upon a free being; it is as unjust to possess a woman exclusively as to possess slaves; all men are born free, all are equal in law; let us never lose sight of these principles; for this reason the right can never be given to one sex to take possession of the other; and never can one of the sexes or classes have an arbitrary right over the other. In the pure state of Nature's laws, a woman cannot even allege in refusal of one who desires her that she loves another, for this becomes a reason for exclusion; and no man can be excluded from the enjoyment of a woman when it becomes clear that she belongs to all men. The act of possession can only be exercised upon a piece of furniture or an animal; it can never be used upon a human being of our own kind; and any tie you may imagine which can bind a woman to a man is as unjust as it is fantastic.

If, then, it appears beyond contradiction that Nature has given us the right to carry out our wishes upon all women indifferently, it appears equally that we have the right to force her to submit to our wishes, not in exclusivity, for them I would contradict myself, but momentarily.[4] It is beyond question that we have the right to establish laws which will force woman to yield to the ardors of him who desires her; violence itself being one of the results of this right, we can legally employ it. Has not Nature proved to us that we have this right, by allotting us the strength

[4] Let no one say at this point that I am contradicting myself, and that having established above that we have no right to bind a woman to ourselves, I now destroy this principle by saying that we have the right to force her; I repeat that it is not a question of property but of enjoyment; I have no right to the ownership of the fountain that lies in my path, but I certainly have the right to make use of it; I have the right to enjoy the limpid water offered up to my thirst; in the same way I have no actual claim to the possession of such and such a woman, but I have an incontestable one to the enjoyment of her; and I have the right to force her to this enjoyment if she refuses me for any motive whatsoever.

necessary to force them to our desires?

In vain may women protest modesty or attachment to other men in their defence; these chimerical reasons count for nothing; we have already seen that modesty is an artificial and despicable emotion. Neither has love, which might be called *madness of the soul*, any right to justify their fidelity; it satisfies only two individuals, the beloved and the lover, and cannot therefore increase the happiness of others; but women were given to us for the general happiness, not for an egotistical and privileged enjoyment. All men, then, have an equal right to the enjoyment of all women; and there is no man, according to Nature's laws, who can institute a unique and personal claim to any woman. The law which will oblige them to prostitute themselves in the brothels I have spoken of, which will force them if they evade it, is therefore the most equitable of laws and one against which no legitimate excuse can be urged.

A man who wishes to enjoy any woman or girl may thus, if you pass just laws, summon her to appear in one of the houses I have described; and there, safeguarded by the matrons of this temple of Venus, she will be offered in complete meekness and submission to satisfy all the caprices he wishes to indulge with her, however strange and irregular they may be, for there is none that is not inspired by Nature, none that she can refuse. It would only remain then to fix the age; but I claim that that cannot be done without hampering the freedom of whoever desires a girl of such and such an age.

Whoever has the right to eat the fruit off a tree may assuredly pluck it either ripe or green according to his taste. But it will be objected that at this age the interference of a man will have a decisively bad effect on the health of the child. That consideration is meaningless: once you have accorded me the right to enjoyment, this right is independent of the effects of the enjoyment; from that moment on, it makes no difference whether the act of enjoyment is beneficial or harmful to the object submitting to it. Have I not already proved that it would be legal to force a woman, and that as soon as she kindles a desire to enjoy her, she must submit to being enjoyed without any egotistical considerations?

It is the same with her health. The moment that the enjoyment of him who desires and has the right to take possession is spoiled or weakened by such considerations, the question of age must be forgotten; for we are not concerned with the sensations of the object condemned by Nature and the law to assuage momentarily another's desires; we are only concerned in this analysis with what pleases the one who desires. We shall redress the balance.

Yes, it shall be redressed, it undoubtedly must be; these women that we have served so cruelly must certainly be recompensed; and this is going to form the reply to the second question I asked.

If we admit, as we have just done, that all women should submit to our desires, surely we should also allow them fully to satisfy their own; our laws should in this respect look favorably upon their ardent natures; and it is absurd that we have assigned both their honor and their virtue to the unnatural strength they must use to resist the inclinations with which they have been far more profusely endowed than we. This social injustice is even more glaring since we agree both to weaken them by our seduction and then to punish them when they yield to all our efforts to make them fall. The whole absurdity of our morals, it seems to me, is contained in that atrocious injustice, and the revelation of that alone should be enough to make us realize the absolute necessity of changing it for purer morality.

I claim that women, who have far more violent desires than we for the pleasures of lust, should be able to express them as much as they wish, free from the bonds of marriage, from all the false prejudices of modesty, completely returned to the state of Nature. I want the law to permit them to enjoy as many men as they like; I want the enjoyment of both sexes and all part of their bodies to be allowed to them as to men; and under the ruling that they suffer themselves to be enjoyed by whoever wants them, they must also be allowed the freedom to enjoy whoever they think is capable of satisfying them.

What, I ask you, are the dangers of such license? Children without a father? What does this matter in a republic, where citizens should have no mother but their country, where all infants are born children of their country! How much greater will be their love for their country when they have known no other mother, when they know they must look to their country for everything! Do not imagine you can make good republicans by isolating children in their families when they should belong only to the republic. By giving their affection to a few individuals instead of to all their fellow men, they inevitably adopt the often dangerous prejudices of these individuals; their ideas and opinions isolate them, characterize them, and all the virtues of a citizen escape them completely. They give their whole heart to those who brought them into the world and have no affection left for the country that teaches them to live, to understand themselves, and make their name – as though these latter benefits were not more important that the former! If it is to our great disadvantage to let infants imbibe the interests of the family and not the very different ones of the mother country, then it is indeed to our advantage to separate them from the family; and this would happen naturally under the conditions I have outlined; for by completely destroying the bonds of marriage, the fruit of pleasure in women would be children forbidden any knowledge of their fathers and thus prevented from belonging to a family, instead of being, as they should, children of their country alone.

We will, then, have brothels destined for the concupiscence of women; like those for men, they will be under the protection of the government; there, all the individuals of either sex that they might desire will be supplied, and the more they frequent these houses the more they will be respected. Nothing is so barbarous and ridiculous as the fact that we have identified woman's virtue and honor with the resistance she employs against the desires she has received from Nature and which burn continually in those who have the barbarity to condemn her for submitting to them. From the most tender age,[5] therefore, a young girl who is free from a father's care, having no need to save herself for marriage – completely abolished by the wise laws I advocate, free from the prejudice that has enslaved her sex, will be able to surrender herself to all that her temperament commands, in places devoted to this subject; there she will be received with respect, satisfied in profusion, and on her return to society she can speak as publicly of the pleasure she has tasted as today she speaks of a ball or an excursion. Fair sex, you will be free; you will enjoy, as men do, all the pleasures that are your duty to Nature; you will stop at nothing. Must one half of humanity chain the diviner half? Oh, break the chains, Nature commands it; know no other curb but your preferences, no other laws but your desires, no other morality but Nature's; no longer languish beneath those savage prejudices that wither your charms, fetter the divine impulses of your hearts;[6] you are as free as we are, and the career of Venus' battles is open to you as to us; no longer fear absurd reproaches; pedantry and superstition are overthrown; we will never again see you blush at your charming excesses; crowned with myrtle and roses, our esteem for you will be the greater as you give these excesses yet wider scope.

[5] Babylonian females did not wait till the age of seven to bring their first fruits to the temple of Venus. The first stirring of desire that a girl feels is the moment that Nature means her to prostitute herself, and with no other consideration in mind, she should obey Nature's voice; she outrages her laws if she resists them.

[6] Women do not realize how much their sensualities embellish them. Compare two women of about the same age and beauty, one of whom lives in celibacy and the other in libertinism; you will see how the latter takes the prize for brilliance and bloom; any transgression against Nature is more aging than an excess of pleasures; and everyone knows that confinements make a woman more beautiful.

Our foregoing analysis obviously makes it unnecessary to discuss adultery; let us glance at it, nevertheless, however meaningless it becomes after the laws I have established. How ridiculous it was to consider it a crime under our former institutions! If there was one thing in the world particularly absurd it was the eternal duration of the marriage bond; one had surely only to observe or experience the weight of these chains to cease to consider any alleviating action a crime; and Nature, as we have remarked, having endowed women with a more passionate temperament and greater sensibility than the other sex, the marriage bond was undoubtedly more stifling for them.

Ardent women, on fire with the flames of love, recompense yourselves now without fear; realize that there cannot be any harm in following Nature's impulses, that she did not create you for one man but for the delight of all. Let nothing restrain you. Imitate the Greek republicans; their legislators never dreamed of making adultery a crime, and they nearly all authorized women's excesses. Thomas More in his Utopia proves that it is advantageous to a woman to give herself up to debauchery, and this great man's ideas were not always mere fantasy.[7]

Among the Tartars, the more a woman prostituted herself the more she was honored; she showed the marks of her immodesty openly on her neck; and a woman with none of these decorations was considered worthless. In Pegu, wives and daughters are lent by the family to passing travelers; they are hired out at so much a day like horses or carriages! Volumes could be written to prove that sexual indulgence was never considered criminal among any of the wiser nations. Every philosopher realizes that we have only the Christian impostors to thank for making it a crime. The priests had a good reason for forbidding us indulgence; this command, by keeping the knowledge and absolution of these secret sins for them alone, gave them unbelievable power over women and opened the way to a life of unlimited lust. We know how they profited by it and how they would still if they had not irretrevably lost their credit.

Is incest more dangerous? Undoubtedly not; it extends the family ties and consequently makes the citizen's love of his country more active; it is commanded us by Nature's first laws; we feel the necessity of it; and it makes the enjoyment of objects that belong to us seem yet more delicious. The earliest institutions favored incest; it is found in primitive societies; it has been con-

---

[7] He also suggested that betrothed couples should see each other naked before marrying. How many marriages would not take place if this law were enforced! It will be admitted that otherwise it is a case of what we call buying a pig in a poke.

secrated by all religions, and favored by all laws. If we survey the whole world we see that incest has been established everywhere. The Negroes of the Pepper Coast and the Gaboon pimp for their wives to their own children; the eldest son of Judah had to marry his father's wife; the peoples of Chile sleep with sisters or daughters indifferently and marry mother and daughter at the same time. To put it briefly, I dare affirm that incest should be the rule under any government based on fraternity. How could reasonable men go to the absurd lengths of thinking that the enjoyment of mother, sister, or daughter could ever be a crime? I ask you, is it not abominably prejudiced to make a man a criminal if he enhances his appreciation of the object closest to him by ties of Nature! It is like saying that we are forbidden to love too much just those individuals whom Nature teaches us to love the most, and that the more she inclines us towards an object, the more she also bids us keep our distance. These contradictions are absurd; only races debased by superstition could believe in them or adopt them. Since the communal state of women that I propose would necessarily involve incest, there is little more to say about this supposed crime that is so obviously a fallacy; and we will pass to rape, which seems at first sight to be the most clearly injurious of all forms of libertinism because of its apparent outrage. It is nevertheless certain that rape, so rare and hard to prove, does less harm than robbery, for the latter appropriates the property, while the former only spoils it. And how could you answer a violator if he objected that in fact he had done but slight harm, since he had only made a certain alteration in an object which would soon have have been made in any case through marriage or desire?

But sodomy, then, this so-called crime which brought the wrath of heaven upon the cities given over to it, is this not a monstrous perversion that cannot be too severely punished? It is undoubtedly painful for us to have to reproach our ancestors with the legal murders which they permitted for this cause. Is it possible to be so uncivilized as to condemn an unfortunate individual to death because he has different tastes from ours? It makes one shudder to realize that our legislators were still at that point less than forty years ago. Have no fear, Citizens; such absurdities will not happen again; the wisdom of your legislators will see to that. Now that we are enlightened on this subject of the weakness of certain men, we realize today that such a weakness cannot be criminal, and that Nature could not attach enough importance to the fluid in our loins to be angry over which channel we choose to direct it into.

What is the only crime that can exist here? It is assuredly not in placing oneself in one particular place or another, unless one tries to maintain that the different parts of the body are not really all exactly the same and that some are pure and some filthy; but since it is impossible to put forward such absurdities, the only so-called crime in this case must be the actual loss of semen. Now I ask you, is it likely that that semen is so precious in Nature's eyes that in releasing it one commits a crime? Would she permit this release every day if that were so? Does she not authorize it by permitting the semen to escape during dreams or during the enjoyment of a pregnant woman? Is it conceivable that Nature would enable us to commit a crime that outraged her? Could she consent to men destroying her pleasures and so becoming stronger than she? We fall into an endless gulf of absurdities if we thus abandon the light of reason in our arguments. Let us rest assured, therefore, that it is as natural to have a woman in one way as in another, that it is absolutely indifferent whether we enjoy a boy or a girl, and that once it is agreed that no other desires can exist in us but those received from Nature, Nature herself is too wise and too logical to implant in us anything that could offend her.

The taste for sodomy is the result of our constitution, which we do not foster in vain. Children show this preference from a tender age and never swerve from it. Sometimes it is the fruit of satiety; but even then, is it not still a part of Nature? From every point of view, it is Nature's handiwork, and all that she inspires must be viewed with respect. If it could be proved, by taking an exact census, that this taste is infinitely more widespread than the other, that its pleasures are far keener, and that for this reason its supporters are far more numerous than its enemies, might it not be possible to conclude that this vice, far from outraging Nature, accords with her purposes, and that she is far less concerned with reproduction than we foolishly believe. If we take the whole world into consideration, how many peoples do we see who despise women! Some of them will have nothing to do with women except to get a child to succeed them. In a republic the custom of men living side by side always makes this vice more frequent, but it is not dangerous. Would the legislators of Greece have introduced it into their republic if they had thought so? Far from it, they thought it necessary in a fighting nation. Plutarch tells us with enthusiasm of the battalion of the *lovers and the beloved:* they alone continued to defend the liberty of Greece. This vice reigned in a society of brothers in arms; it strengthened it. The greatest men have been interested in it. The whole of America, when it was discovered, was peopled with men with these inclinations. Among the Illinois in Louisiana, men dressed as women prostituted themselves like courtesans. The Negroes of Bengela openly had relations with men; in Algeria, nearly all the seraglios today are wholly populated by young boys. In Thebes, the love of boys was not only tolerated but recommended; the Cheronean philosopher advised it to sweeten the love of young men.

We know to what extent it held sway in Rome; there were public places where young boys prostituted themselves in the disguise of women, and girls in the dress of boys. Martial, Catullus, Tibullus, Horace, and Virgil wrote to men in the terms used to a mistress; and we read in Plutarch[8] that women should have no part in the love of men. The Amasians on the island of Crete used to carry off young boys with unusual ceremonies. When someone was attracted by a boy, the parents were informed of the day the seducer intended to take him away; the youth put up some resistance if he did not like his lover; otherwise he went off with him, and the seducer sent him back to his family as soon as he had had enough; for with this passion as with the love of women, to have enough is to have too much.

Strabo tells us that on the same island the seraglios contained only boys; they were publicly prostituted.

Is another authority needed to prove how useful this vice is in a republic? Listen to Jerome the Peripatetic: the love of boys, he says, spread throughout Greece, for it gave us courage and strength and helped to expel the tyrants. Pacts were formed among the lovers, and they would rather be tortured than reveal their accomplices; thus patriotism sacrificed everything for the good of the state; it was certain that these bonds strengthened the republic; women were inveighed against, and it became a weakness characteristic of tyrants to attach oneself to such creatures. Homosexuality was always the vice of warlike nations. Caesar tells us that the Gauls were very much given to it. The wars which a republic had to undertake encouraged this vice by separating the sexes; and when it was realized that this result was so useful to the state, religion soon blessed it. It is known that the Romans consecrated the love of Jupiter and Ganymede. Sextus Empiricus assures us that this inclination was enforced among the Persians. Finally the women, jealous and despised, offered their husbands the same service that boys gave them; some tried this and returned to their former habits, finding the illusion impossible to sustain.

The Turks, greatly given to this perversion which is blessed in the Koran, assert nevertheless that a very young virgin can take the place of a boy; and their females seldom become women without having passed this ordeal. Sixtus V and Sanchez permitted this license; the latter even undertook to prove that it was advantag-

[8] *Moralia*, treatise on love.

eous to propagation and that a child conceived after this preliminary was infinitely the better for it. The women made amends among themselves. This diversion certainly has no more drawbacks than the other, for the result is only a refusal to propagate, and the power of those who have the taste for reproduction is too strong to be destroyed by its adversaries. The Greeks even supported this perversion of women for reasons of state. It had the result that women were satisfied with each other, and since their communications with men were less frequent, they meddled less in the affairs of the republic. Lucian tells us what progress was made by this license, and it is not without interest that we observe it in Sappho.

In a word, there is no danger at all in any of these manias; should they go even further, to the caresses of monsters and animals, which we notice in the history of all nations, there would not be the slightest danger in any of these whims; for corrupt habits, often very useful to a government, cannot injure it in any way; and we must expect enough wisdom and prudence from our legislators to be sure that they will issue no law repressing these peculiarities, which are an inextricable part of the individual constitution and could no more be laid to the guilt of the owner than a congenital deformity.

There remains only murder to be examined under the second group of crimes against our fellow men, and then we will pass to man's obligations to himself. Of all man's offenses against his fellow man, murder is without contradiction the cruelest, for it deprives him of the one gift he has received from Nature, the only one whose loss is irreparable. Nevertheless several questions arise at this point, apart from the wrong which murder does to its victim.

1. Considering Nature's laws only, is it really criminal?
2. Is it criminal in relation to the laws of politics?
3. It is harmful to society?
4. How should it be considered in a republican state?
5. Finally, should murder be punished by murder?

We will examine each of these questions separately; the object is important enough to allow us to linger; our ideas will perhaps be found somewhat strong, but what matter? Have we not gained the right to say all we wish? Let us reveal great truths to men; they expect them from us; error must be dissipated, its blindfold must fall beside that of kings. Is murder a crime in Nature's eyes? Such is the first question.

We are doubtless now going to humiliate man's pride by reducing him to the stature of all the other productions of Nature;

but the philosopher does not pander to trivial human vanities; ardent in the pursuit of truth, he extricates it from the crass prejudices of self-love, grasps it, develops it, and bravely shows it to the astonished world.

What is man, and what difference is there between him and the other plants, the other animals of the earth? None, certainly. Fortuitously situated, like them, on this earth, he is born like them, propagates, grows, withers like them; he reaches old age, and like them falls into nothingness after the span assigned to each species by Nature according to its physical characteristics. If these similarities are such that the scrutinizing eye of the philosopher can perceive no difference, then there is just as much harm in killing an animal as a man, or just as little, and the difference arises solely from the prejudices of our vanity; unfortunately nothing is more absurd than the prejudices of vanity. But let us take the question further. You cannot disagree that it is the same to kill a man or an animal; but is not the destruction of any living creature wrong, as the Pythagoreans believed and as some dwellers on the banks of the Ganges still believe? Before replying let us remind the reader that we are only examining the question in relation to Nature; we will consider it later with regard to men.

Now I ask you how valuable can creatures be to Nature that cost her neither trouble nor care? The workman only values his handiwork because of the work he put into it, because of the time spent in creating it. Does man cost Nature anything? And if he does cost her something, is it more than a monkey or an elephant? I will go further; what are the regenerative materials of Nature? What are newborn creatures created from? Do not the three elements of which they are made come originally from the destruction of other bodies? If every individual were eternal, would it not become impossible for Nature to create new ones? If eternal life is impossible for living things, their destruction is one of Nature's laws.

If this destruction is so necessary to Nature that it is impossible for her to do without it, and if she cannot create without drawing on the mass of dead matter prepared for her by death, then the idea of annihilation which we associate with death becomes meaningless; there will be no more simple annihilation; what we call the end of a living creature will no longer be the actual end but a mere transmutation of matter, which is accepted by all modern thinkers as one of the first laws. Death, according to these irrefutable principles, is only a change of form, an imperceptible transition from one existence to another, which is what

Pythagoras called metempsychosis.

Once these truths are admitted, can one possibly maintain that destruction is a crime? Do you care to say, for the sake of preserving your absurd prejudices, that transmutation is the same as destruction? Certainly not, for you would have to prove that matter underwent a moment of inaction, a time of quiescence. This you will never discover. Small animals come into being the moment a large animal breathes its last, and the life of these tiny creatures is only a necessary and inevitable result of the temporary sleep of the greater. Can you venture to say at this time that one is more pleasing to Nature than the other? You would have to prove an impossibility – that a long or square shape is more pleasing or useful to Nature than an oblong or triangular one; you would have to prove that even in view of Nature's sublime plans, a sluggard who grows fat in idleness and inaction is more useful to Nature than the horse, whose service is so essential, or the ox, whose body is so precious that every part of it can be used; you would have to prove that the venomous serpent is more necessary than the faithful dog.

Now, since all these propositions are untenable, we must agree to admit the impossibility of destroying any of Nature's works; that given the assurance that the only thing we are doing in allowing ourselves to destroy is to make a change in the forms of things, but without extinguishing life, then it is beyond human power to prove that there is any crime in the so-called destruction of a creature, of any age, sex, or species you can imagine. To follow the train of consequences yet further, and linking one event to another, we see that the action of altering the forms of Nature is beneficial to her, since it produces the material for her reconstructions which would be impossible for her if nothing were destroyed, Well, let her do it herself! you will be told. Certainly let her do it. but it is at her inspiration that man gives way to murder; it is Nature that prompts him, and the man who destroys his fellow is to Nature what a plague or famine is, sent by her hand in the same way, for she uses all possible means to obtain the raw material of destruction so essential to her work. Let us vouchsafe for a moment to illumine our minds with the holy light of philosophy; what other voice but Nature's suggests to us the personal hatreds, vengeances, wars, in fact all the eternal motives for murder? Then if she prompts them, it is because she needs them. How, in that case, can we imagine that we are guilty towards her, when we are only following her wishes?

This is already more than sufficient to convince any enlightened reader that murder could never be an offense against Nature.

Is it a political crime? Let us frankly admit that it is, on the contrary, one of the greatest powers in politics. Was it not through murders that Rome became mistress of the world? Is it not by means of murders that France has freed herself today? It is useless to say that we are now speaking of murders caused by war and not of atrocities committed by the seditious and rebellious; the former was worthy of public execration and need only be remembered to excite general horror and indignation. What human science most needs to be maintained by massacre? Only one that sets out to deceive itself, which aims at the aggrandizement of one nation at the expense of another. Are wars, the sole fruit of this uncivilized policy, anything but the means of fostering, defending, and supporting it? And what is war but the science of destruction? What a strange lack of insight we show by publicly teaching the art of killing, rewarding the most successful, and then punishing whoever is revenged on his enemy in a personal matter. Is it not time to change such barbarous errors?

Is murder, then, a crime against society? Who could seriously imagine so! What does it matter to a populous society whether there is one member more or less in its midst? Are its laws, morals, or customs thereby weakened? Can the death of an individual ever have any influence on the mass of people? And after the losses of a great battle – or I may as well say after the extinction of half the population, or the whole of it, if you like – would the few beings left alive experience the slightest material alteration? Alas, no; nor would the whole of Nature experience any alteration; and the stupid pride of mankind, that believes that everything was created for itself, would be astonished to realize that after the total destruction of the human race nothing in Nature was changed nor the stars slowed down in their courses. But let us proceed.

How should murder be viewed in a martial republican state?

It would undoubtedly be thoroughly dangerous either to look unfavorably on this action or to punish it. The pride of the republican demands a certain amount of ferocity; if he becomes soft and loses his power, he will soon be subjugated. A strange idea becomes apparent at this point; but since it is true as well as daring, I will voice it. A nation that starts as a republic can only maintain itself by the virtues, for to arrive at the greater, one must start with the lesser; but a nation that is already old and corrupt, and bravely throws off the yoke of monarchist government to adopt the republican rule, can only maintain itself by crimes; for it is already criminal; and to pass from crime to virtue, from a violent state to a quiet one, would be to fall into an inertia which would quickly result in ruin. What would become of a tree transplanted from fertile ground to a dry sandy soil? All intellectual ideas are so subordinated to physical nature that a comparison with growing things will always provide a moral guide.

Savages, the most independent of men and the nearest to Nature, every day indulge in murder with impunity. In Sparta and Lacedaemon they hunted slaves as we hunt partridges. The freest peoples are those who look on this with most favor. In Mindanao, the boy who wishes to commit a murder is elevated to the ranks of the brave, and is decorated with a turban; among the Caraguos, seven men must be killed before obtaining this headdress; the natives of Borneo believe that those they put to death will have to serve them when they are dead themselves; even the pious Spaniards made a vow to Saint James of Galicia to kill twelve American natives a day; in the kingdom of Tangut, a strong and vigorous young man is chosen and permitted on certain days of the year to kill everyone he meets! Was there ever a race more sympathetic to murder than the Jews? It appears in all forms on every page of their history.

The emperor and mandarins of China occasionally take measures to make the people revolt, so that they can have an excuse for affecting a dreadful slaughter. Should this meek and effeminate nation free itself from the yoke of its tyrants, it will slaughter them in turn, with better cause, and murder, once again found necessary and adopted, will only have changed its victims; it was first the enjoyment of one side and it will become the pastime of the other.

An infinite number of nations tolerate public assassination; it is openly allowed in Genoa, Venice, Naples, and the whole of Albania; at Kachao, on the San Domingo River, assassins dressed in a well-known and recognized uniform, will butcher according to orders, before your very eyes, whatever individual you name. The Indians take opium to spur themselves on to murder, then rush into the streets and massacre everyone they meet; English travelers have observed this mania in Batavia.

What other nation has ever been both as great and as cruel as the Romans, and what other nation has kept its splendor and freedom for so long? The gladiatorial shows sustained their courage: they became warlike through the custom of making a game of killing. Twelve or fifteen hundred victims filled the circus arena every day; and there the women, more cruel than the men, dared to demand that the dying men fall gracefully and strike an attitude even in the throes of death. The Romans went from this to the pleasures of watching dwarfs slaughter each other; and when the Christian cult infected the earth and persuaded men that

111

killing was an evil, the Romans were at once enslaved by tyrants, and the heroes of the world soon became its playthings.

All over the world, in fact, it has been rightly believed that the murderer, that is to say, the man who stifles his sensibility to the point of killing his fellow man and defying public or private vengeance, must be very brave and therefore very valuable to a warlike or republican society. If we glance at nations who are fiercer still and do not stop at sacrificing children, often their own, we see that these actions are universally adopted, sometimes even embodied in the laws. Many savage tribes kill their children as soon as they are born. On the banks of the Orinoco River, mothers used to sacrifice female children as soon as they had brought them into the world, for they were convinced their daughters were only born to be unhappy, destined to be married in a region where women were scarcely tolerated. In Trapobania and the kingdom of Sopit, all deformed children were killed by their own parents.

The women of Madagascar exposed all children born on certain days of the week to the attacks of wild animals. In the Greek republics all newborn children were carefully examined, and if they were not found to be formed well enough to defend their republic some day, they were immediately destroyed; it was not considered necessary to erect lavishly endowed institutions[9] to preserve this vile scum of human nature. Up until the removal of the seat of empire, all Romans who did not want to bring up their children threw them into the sewer. The legislators of the ancient world did not scruple to condemn infants to death, and none of their codes put any check on the rights which a father considered he held over his family. Aristotle advised abortion; and these republicans of the old days, filled with enthusiasm and ardor for their country, did not know the individual sympathy found in modern nations: they loved their children less, but they loved their country more. In every town in China an incredible number of abandoned children are found in the streets every day; a cart collects them at dawn, and they are thrown into a ditch; often the midwives themselves rid the mothers of them by immediately suffocating their offspring in tubs of boiling water or by throwing them into a stream.

At Peking they are put into little rush baskets and left on the canals; these canals are scoured every day, and the famous traveler Duhalde estimates the number picked up each day at more

[9] It is hoped that the nation will do away with this expense, the most unnecessary one of all; any individual born without the necessary qualities to serve the republic later on has no right to life; and the best thing to do is to take it from him as soon as he receives it.

than thirty thousand. It cannot be denied that it would be very necessary and extremely useful to put a limit to the population in a republican state; from an opposite point of view, the population should be encouraged in a monarchy: there the tyrants, rich only in proportion to the number of their slaves, certainly need more men; but an overabundant population, make no mistake about it, is a real evil in a republican state; nevertheless there is no need to slaughter in order to reduce it, as some of our modern decemvirs would; it is only a question of not allowing it to spread beyond the bounds that well-being prescribes. Take care not to multiply a population where every man is a king; and realize that revolutions are always the natural result of too large a population.

If, for the glory of the state, you give your soldiers the right to destroy men, then for the preservation of this same state, give each individual an equal right to destroy, wherever he can without outraging Nature, children that he cannot bring up, or who will bring no support to the country; allow him also to rid himself at his own risk of all the enemies who might injure him; for the result of all these actions, meaningless in themselves, will be to keep the population in check, and never numerous enough to overthrow your government. Let monarchists say that a state is only great according to the size of its population: the state will always be poor if its population exceeds its means of supporting life, and it will always flourish if it is kept within limits and can trade its superfluous goods. Do you not prune a tree when it has too many branches? Do you not clip the branches to preserve the trunk? Any system that departs from these principles is an extravagance and a source of abuses that will soon lead to the total overthrow of the structure we have erected with so much labor; but it is not the full-grown man we should destroy in order to decrease the population. It is unfair to cut short the life of a fully formed individual; but it is not so, I maintain, to prevent a creature who is certain to have no use in life from growing up. The human race should be thinned out from the cradle; the being that you realize can never be useful to society is the one whose life should be cut short at the breast; these are the only reasonable ways of diminishing a population whose increase would, as I have proved, become a most dangerous abuse.

Now let us resume our argument.

Should murder be punished by murder? Certainly not. Let us impose no punishment on the murderer but the risk he incurs from the vengeance of the friends or relatives of the murdered man. *I give you my pardon,* said Louis XV to Charolais, who had killed a man for amusement, *but I also give it to the man who kills you*. The whole foundation of the law against murderers is contained in that sublime saying. [10]

To sum up, murder is a horror, but often a necessary horror and never a criminal one and it must be tolerated in a republican state. I have shown that the whole universe gives us examples of this; but must it be considered an action punishable by death?

Those who can solve the following problem will have answered the question:

Is crime a crime or not?

If it is not, why make laws to punish it?

If it is, by what barbarous and idiotic illogicality do you punish it by a similar crime?

It now remains to discuss man's duties towards himself. Since the philosopher only adopts such duties inasmuch as they minister to his pleasure or self-preservation, it is useless to recommend their adoption or to impose penalties if they are not observed.

The only crime of this type that a man could commit would be suicide. I shall not amuse myself here by pointing out the imbecility of people who make that action into a crime; I shall send anyone without doubts on the matter to Rousseau's famous letter. Almost all the governments of the ancient world authorized suicide on political or religious grounds. The Athenians disclosed to the Areopagus their reasons for killing themselves; then they stabbed themselves. All the Greek republics tolerated suicide; it was a part of the scheme of the ancient legislators; people killed themselves in public and made a formal ceremony of death.

The republic of Rome encouraged suicide; the famous sacrifices for the motherland were simply suicides. When Rome was taken by the Gauls, the most illustrious senators vowed themselves to death; by adopting the same attitude we shall acquire the same virtues. A soldier killed himself, during the campaign of '92, for sheer grief at not being able to follow his comrades at Jemappes. If we are constantly measured against these proud republicans, we shall soon surpass their virtues: the government makes the man. The agelong habit of despotism has sapped our courage completely; our ways have become depraved; but we are being born again; soon it will be seen what sublime actions the French genius and character are capable of when they are free; let us maintain, at the cost of our fortunes and our lives, that liberty that has already

[10] The Salic law punished murder only by a fine; and since the guilty man could easily find a means of avoiding it, Childebert, King of Austrasia, decreed in a ruling made at Cologne a punishment of death, not against murderers, but against anyone who evaded a fine imposed on a murderer. The Ripuarian law also imposed only a fine for this action, graded according to the individual who had been killed. It was very expensive for a priest: a leaden tunic was made to fit the assassin, and he had to pay in gold an equivalent of the weight of the tunic, otherwise he and his family became slaves of the Church.

cost us so many victims, let us not regret one of them if we reach our goal: they gave themselves to it voluntarily; let us not allow that blood to have been spilt in vain; but let us unite ... unite, or we will lose the fruit of all our labors; let us now try to make fine laws after the victories we have won; our first legislators, still enslaved to the despot we have laid low, have given us laws worthy of the tyrant whom they still flatter: let us refashion their work and remember that we are working for republicans now, let our laws be as mild as the people they govern.

In disclosing here, as I have done, the nullity, the indifference of an infinite number of actions that our ancestors, misled by a false religion, believed to be criminal, I am reducing our task to a very simple one. Let us make few laws, but good ones – it is not a question of multiplying restraints but of making those we do employ quite indestructible – let the laws that we promulgate have no other object than the peace and happiness of the citizen and the glory of the republic; but after expelling the enemy from your soil, Frenchmen, I hope that your ardor to propagate your ideas will not take you any further; you can take them to the ends of the earth only by fire and sword. Before carrying out such resolutions, think of the failure of the crusades. When the enemy is on the other side of the Rhine, then, believe me, you must protect your frontiers and stay at home; reorganize your commerce, put energy into manufacturing, and find markets for your goods; let your arts flourish once again; encourage agriculture, which is necessary to a government such as yours and which should provide enough for everyone without the help of anyone else; leave the thrones of Europe to crumble away by themselves; your example and prosperity will soon overthrow them without the need for you to interfere.

Unassailable in your domestic policy, and a model among nations for your police and your wise laws, there will be no government that does not strive to imitate you, none that will not be honored by alliance with you; but if, for the useless honor of spreading your principles abroad, you abandon the study of your own prosperity, then despotism will wake again from its half-sleep, internal dissensions will rend you apart, you will exhaust your finances and your soldiers, and all that only to go back to kissing the chains that will be laid on you again by tyrants during your absence; all that you want can be done without leaving your homes: let other nations see that you are happy, and they will hasten to happiness by the trail that you have blazed for them.

MADAME DE SAINT-ANGE: Well, my dear love, to reward you today for your exquisite kindness, I am handing over to your ardent attentions a young virgin, more beautiful than Venus.

THE CHEVALIER: What! With Dolmancé! You bring a woman to your place?

MADAME DE SAINT-ANGE: It is a question of education; it's a girl I knew at the convent last autumn while my husband was at the spa. We could do nothing there, as too many eyes were on us, but we promised to meet as soon as it became possible; and wholly taken up with this desire, I made the acquaintance of her family to satisfy it. Her father is a rake . . . I won him. At last the beautiful girl came, and I was waiting. We spent two days together, two delightful days, and for the better part of this time I was engaged in educating this young person. Dolmancé and I placed all the wildest principles of libertinism in this head. We burned her with our fires, we fed her with our philosophy, and as I wanted to add something practical to our theorizing, I have appointed you, brother, to gather the myrtles of Cytherea, and Dolmancé the roses of Sodom. I shall have two pleasures at once, that of enjoying these criminal pleasures, and that of giving instruction, of inspiring such tastes in the agreeable innocent I have lured into our nets. Well, Chevalier, is this a plan worthy of my imagination?

THE CHEVALIER: It alone could conceive it; it is divine, sister, and I promise to fill the charming role you have allotted me most wonderfully well. Ah, you rogue! The pleasures you are going to enjoy in educating this child! Wha: delights for you, corrupting her, stifling in that young heart every seed of virtue and religion her teachers have planted! Really, this far too roué for me.

MADAME DE SAINT-ANGE: It is very certain that I will spare nothing to pervert her, degrade her, and overthrow in her all the false moral principles which may have already numbed her. In two lessons I will make her as vicious as I am, as impious, and as debauched. Warn Dolmancé, tell him all the moment he arrives, so that the poison of his immoralities, circulating with mine in that young heart, will quickly uproot the seed of virtue, which might germinate without us.

THE CHEVALIER: You would never find a better man for your plan; irreligion, godlessness, inhumanity, libertinism, all flow from Dolmancé's lips as in other times mystical unction from the lips of the famous Archbishop of Cambrai. He is the soundest seducer, the most corrupted of men, the most dangerous. . . . Ah, my dear friend, if your pupil but responds to her teacher, I can guarantee her lost.

MADAME DE SAINT-ANGE: It will certainly not be long with the gifts I know him to have.

THE CHEVALIER: But tell, dear sister, do you fear nothing from her parents? Suppose the girl talked when she returned home?

MADAME DE SAINT-ANGE: Fear nothing, I have seduced her father. . . . He is mine. Must I confess? I abandoned myself to him so that he would close his eyes; he is unaware of my schemes, but he would never dare get to the core of them . . . I have him.

THE CHEVALIER: Your methods are horrifying!

MADAME DE SAINT-ANGE That is how they must be to be infallible.

THE CHEVALIER: But tell me: who is this young person?

MADAME DE SAINT-ANGE: She is called Eugénie; she is the daughter of one Mistival, one of the richest tax collectors of the capital, about thirty-six years old. Her mother is thirty-two at the most, and the daughter fifteen. Mistival is as rakish as his wife is religious. As for Eugénie, my friend, it would be wasted effort to try and depict her for you. She is far beyond my powers; let it be sufficient to say that neither you nor I have seen anything so delightful in this world. Her hair is chestnut . . . and descends to the base of her rump, her skin is dazzling white, her nose rather aquiline, her eyes ebony black and of such fire! Oh, my friend, it is impossible to hold such eyes! You cannot imagine all the follies they have driven me to. . . . If you saw the fine brows that crown them. . . . Her mouth is small, her teeth surpassing, and all so fresh! One of her beauties is the elegant way her lovely head rises from her shoulders, and the noble air she has in turning it. . . . Eugénie is big for her age; you would say she was seventeen. Her waist is a model of elegance and slenderness, her bosom delicious. . . . They are certainly the two prettiest little breasts! Scarcely enough to fill the hand, but so soft, so fresh, so white! . . . and if only you had seen how excited she grew in my caress . . . how her big eyes told me the state of her soul! My friend, I do not know what more there is. Ah, but if it is to be judged by what I do know, Olympia never knew a goddess to compare. . . . But I hear her. . . . Leave us, go out through the garden to avoid meeting her, and be punctual at the rendezvous.

THE CHEVALIER: The picture you have just painted will answer for my being precise. Oh heavens, to go, to leave you in the state I am in! Farewell! A kiss, a single kiss, my dear sister, just to satisfy me so far. (*She kisses him . . . and the young man leaves hurriedly.*)

3

EUGÉNIE: One thing disturbs me, dear friend, in what you have just told me. Please explain it to me, as I do not understand it at all. Your husband, you say, does not go about enjoying himself in a way that would result in children. Please, what does he do to you?

MADAME DE SAINT-ANGE: My husband was already an old man when I married him. On the very first night of our wedding festivities, he warned me of his eccentricities, assuring me that for his part he would never interfere with mine. I swore I would obey him, and since then we have both lived in the most delicious freedom from restraint. My husband's preference *consiste à se faire sucer, et voici le très singulier épisode qu'il y joint: pendant que, courbée sur lui, mes fesses d'aplomb sur son visage, je pompe avec ardeur le fourtre de ses couilles, il faut que je luci chie dans la bouche! Il avale!*

EUGÉNIE: What an extraordinary taste!

DOLMANCÉ: No taste should be so qualified, my dear. All are in Nature; it pleased her, in creating mankind, to vary their tastes as their faces, and we should no more be astonished at the variety she has put into our deeds than at the range she has placed in our affections. The caprice your friend has just spoken of is very much á la mode; countless men, principally those of a certain age, are prodigiously given to it. Would you refuse, Eugénie, if someone asked it of you?

EUGÉNIE: (*blushing*): If I follow the maxims instilled into me here, could I refuse such a thing? I only cry mercy for my surprise; it is the first time I have heard of such lasciviousness, and first I must form an idea of it. . . .. But however that may be, my dear, did you gain your freedom by consenting to this kindness?

MADAME DE SAINT-ANGE: Wholly, Eugénie. I on my side did all I wished, and he placed no obstacles in my way. But I did not take a lover; I loved pleasure too much for that. Woe to the woman who clings: one lover is enough to ruin her, while ten acts of libertinism, rehearsed every day, will vanish into the night of silence so soon as they have been consummated. I was rich: I paid young people who had me without knowing who I was; I surrounded myself with delightful valets, who were certain to taste the most exquisite pleasures with me if they were discreet, and sure to be dismissed if they breathed a word. Dear angel, you have no idea of the flood of pleasures I plunged into in this way. That is the conduct I would always prescribe to all women who would follow in my steps. In the twelve years I have been married, I have been had by perhaps ten or twelve thousand individuals . . . and I am thought to be judicious in my choice of company! Another woman would have had lovers; the second one would have ruined her.

EUGÉNIE: This is the most reliable of maxims, and I have made up my mind that it shall be mine. Like you, I must marry a rich man, a man, above all, of eccentricities. . . . But my dear, your husband, being strictly bound to his tastes, does he never demand anything else of you?

MADAME DE SAINT-ANGE: Never once in twelve years has he gone back on his word, except when I have a period. Then a very attractive girl replaces me, and things could never be better.

EUGÉNIE: But doubtless he does not confine himself to this. Do not other things converge from outside to vary his pleasures?

DOLMANCÉ: You may be sure of that, Eugénie; madame's husband is one of the greatest rakes of his century. He spends more than a hundred thousand crowns a year on the obscenities your friend has just depicted.

MADAME DE SAINT-ANGE: To tell the truth, I doubt it myself; but then what are his excesses to me, since their number gives both authority and cover to mine?

4

EUGÉNIE: Tell me, my dear, who was the happy man you made master of your virginity?

MADAME DE SAINT-ANGE: My brother. He had worshiped me from childhood, and from our youngest days, we had often amused one another without reaching the end. I promised him I would surrender myself to him as soon as I was married. I kept my word, and as my husband had fortunately done no damage, he gathered all. We continued to indulge in this intrigue, but without putting either of us to a disadvantage; we nonetheless plunged, each on his own, into the divine welter of lewdness. We even did each other services; I procured him women, he introduced me to men.

EUGÉNIE: What a delightful arrangement! But is not incest a crime?

MADAME DE SAINT-ANGE: Can the sweetest liaisons Nature knows be so regarded, those she lays down for us, those she most advises! Let us reason for a moment, Eugénie: how, after the vast misfortunes our earth has undergone, could the human species reproduce itself other than by incest? Do we not find both example and proof in books honored by Christianity? The families of Adam and Noah – could they perpetuate themselves other than by this means?

119

Search, examine the ways of the universe: you will see incest permitted everywhere, and regarded as a wise rule made to cement family ties. In a word, if love is born of affinity, where could it be more perfect than between brother and sister, between father and daughter? Mistaken politics, the product of fearing to make certain families too powerful, forbids it in our moral code; but let us not delude ourselves to such an extent that we take the law away from Nature, which would be following the dictates of self-interest or ambition; rather let us sound our hearts, to which I always refer our moral pedants; let us enquire of this sacred organ, and we will realize that there is nothing more refined than the carnal liaison of families. Let us stop blinding ourselves to the feelings of a brother for his sister, or a father for his daughter. One and the other are vainly disguised beneath the veil of legitimate fondness; the most violent love is the only feeling that kindles in them, for that is the only one Nature has put in our hearts. So let us double and triple these delightful incests and fear nothing, and believe that the closer the object of our desires, the more charms we shall enjoy in it.

Un de mes amis vit habituellement avec la fille qu'il a eue de sa propre mère; il n'y a pas huit jours qu'il dépucela un garçon de treize ans, fruit de son commerce avec cette fille; dans quelques années ce même jeune homme épousera sa mère. Such are my friend's wishes, and he has in store a fate for them similar to that of his other projects; his intentions, as I know, are to enjoy still more fruits that shall be born of this wedding; he is young and has reason to hope. You see, dearest Eugénie, with what a heap of incests and crimes this good friend of mine would defile himself if there were any truth in the prejudice that makes us see evil in these liaisons. In a word, in such matters I always have one principle as starting point: if Nature forbade sodomitic indulgences, incestuous practices, pollutions, and so on, would she allow us to find so much pleasure in them? It is impossible that she would tolerate what really outrages her.

EUGÉNIE: Oh, heavenly teachers, how well I see that according to your principles, there are very few crimes on earth, and that we can peacefully abandon ourselves to all our desires, however strange they may appear to the fools who, taking offense and alarm at all things, are stupid enough to mistake social institutions for the divine laws of Nature.

EUGÉNIE: Now, sir, how does your philosophy explain this kind of misdemeanor: is it not frightful?

DOLMANCÉ: Begin with this starting point, Eugénie: that in licentiousness nothing is frightful, for all that is inspired by libertinism, is equally so by Nature. The most extraordinary, the most curious acts, those that most obviously offend all the laws and all human institutions (for I cannot speak of heaven), well, Eugénie, even they are not frightful, and there is not one of them that cannot be pointed to in Nature. It is certain that the one of which you speak is the same as is found in a curious story in the tedious romance of Holy Scripture (the tiresome compilation of an ignorant Jew during the captivity of Babylon); but it is false, beyond all probability, that these towns, or rather these villages, perished by fire in punishment for these deviations. Situated on the crater of a number of former volcanoes, Sodom and Gomorrah perished like those Italian towns engulfed in the lava of Vesuvius: there is your miracle; and yet from this quite ordinary event they went on to the barbarous invention of punishment by fire for those unfortunate humans who, in parts of Europe, took to this natural fancy.

EUGÉNIE: Natural! Oh!

DOLMANCÉ: Yes, natural, I insist: Nature has not two voices, one that is daily employed in condemning what the other prompts to do . . . Those who would forbid or condemn this taste claim that it is injurious to the population. What shallow fools they are whose heads are filled with this idea of population, and who see nothing but crime in all that departs from this idea! Has it then been proved that Nature has as great a need of this population as they would lead us to suppose? Is it established that each deviation from this senseless propagation is an outrage? Let us examine its progress and its laws to convince ourselves. If Nature did nothing but create, and if she never destroyed, I might believe with these dull sophists that the most noble of all acts would be to work unceasingly at what produces; and I would agree with them that, this being so, refusal to produce would necessarily be a crime; but the merest glance at Nature – does not this prove that destruction is as necessary to her scheme of things as creation, that these operations, one and the other, are so intimately bound and interlinked that it is impossible for one to take place without the other, that nothing would be born, that there would be no regeneration without destruction? Therefore destruction, like creation, is one of the laws of Nature.

Once this principle is admitted, how can I offend this Nature by refusing to create? Which, supposing this action evil, is no doubt one infinitely less so than destroying, which is nevertheless part of her laws, as I have just proved. If then, on the one hand, I admit the taste Nature gives me for this loss, and see, on the other, that it is necessary to her, and that by indulging it I only share her outlook, where then, I ask you, is the crime? But fools and populators, who are synonymous, claim that this productive sperm is not put in your guts for any other purpose than that of propagation and that to deviate from it is an offense. I have just proved that this is not so, since this waste is not even the equivalent of a destruction, which, far more important than waste, is itself no crime.

In the second place it is not true that Nature destines this spermatic liquid exclusively and entirely to reproduction; if this were so, she would prohibit its discharge under any other circumstance – a fact contrary to our experience, for we lose it where and when we will – and she would oppose such losses outside of coitus, such as do happen both in our dreams and our recollections. Miserly with so precious a liquid, she would only permit discharge in the vase of propagation; she would certainly never permit us to know that pleasure with which she crowns us when we do deviate from our homage, for it would not be reasonable to suppose that she would consent to give us pleasure at the very moment we heap insults on her. Let us go further; if women were born only to bear, which would surely be so if Nature held production so dear, would the longest female life have no more than seven years, all deductions made, in which she was in a condition to give birth to her like? . . . [Man] finds the same pleasure in this loss as in its useful employment, and never the least disadvantage! . . .

Far from outraging Nature, let us believe the contrary, that the sodomite and tribade serve Nature in stubbornly refusing a conjunction that results only in irksome offspring. Let us make no mistake: such propagation was never one of her laws, but was at the very most something tolerated. . . . What matter to her the extinction or destruction of mankind on earth!

Do you believe that there are not already extinct species? Buffon reckons several . . . and the whole race might be annihilated, and the air would be not a whit less pure, the sun less brilliant, the course of the world less true.

But what idiocy it takes to believe that our race is so useful to the world that whoever does not labor to increase it or who disturbs such increase must thereby be a criminal! Let us stop blinding ourselves on this score, and let the example of the most reasonable of peoples persuade us of our errors. There is not a corner of the earth where this supposed crime of sodomy has not had temples and votaries. The Greeks, who, so to speak, made a virtue of it, erected it a statue under the name of Venus Callipyge; Rome went looking for laws at Athens and brought back this divine taste. What progress was made under the emperors! Sheltered by Roman eagles, it ranged from one end of the earth to the other; on the destruction of the empire, it took refuge close to the papacy; it followed the arts in Italy, and came down to us as we became civilized. Whenever we discover a hemisphere, we find sodomy there. Cook drops anchor in a new world, and there it reigns. If our balloons had reached the moon, they would have found it there just the same. Delicious inclination! Child of Nature and of pleasure, you should be everywhere men are, and everywhere you are known, they will raise you altars!

From

JULIETTE

1

'We do punish libertinism,' my tutor [Noirceuil] went on. 'Plutarch tells us that the Samnites went daily, under legal supervision, to a place called "The Gardens," and that there they abandoned themselves pell-mell to such lascivious pleasures that it was almost impossible to imagine them! The historian goes on to say that in this blessed spot the distinctions of sex and the ties of blood vanished beneath the lure of pleasure: *l'ami devenait la femme de son ami; la fille, la tribade de sa mère, et plus souvent encore le fils, la catin de son père, à côté du frère enculant sa soeur.*

'We rate the blushing maiden highly. Not so the Filipinos; in their isles are public officials who are paid well to deflower virgins on their wedding eve.

'In Sparta, adultery was publicly permitted.

'We despise girls who have prostituted themselves. The maidens of Lydia, on the contrary, were only valued in proportion to the number of their lovers. The fruits of their prostitution was their one and only dowry.

'The women of Cyprus, to make money, went to sell themselves in public to every foreigner who landed on their island.

'Moral depravation is necessary in a state; the Romans sensed this in establishing brothels of boys and girls the whole breadth of the republic, and theaters whose girls danced completely naked.

'The women of Babylon prostituted themselves once a year in the temple of Venus; the Armenian women were obliged to dedicate their virginity to the priests of Tanais, who indulged in primitive sodomy with them, allowing them the favor of being deflowered only insofar as they had sustained the earlier attacks stoutheartedly; a protest, a tear, a movement, a cry – if this escaped them, they were deprived of the second attack, and found no further opportunity to marry.

'The Canarians of Goa make their daughters suffer quite a different torture; they prostitute them to an idol fitted with an iron member of prodigious size; they thrust them forcibly upon this terrible *godemiché* that they have taken care to heat wonderfully. In this dilated state the child goes looking for a husband, who will not take her without this ceremony.

'The Cainites, second-century heretics, claimed that heaven was only reached by incontinence. They maintained that each infamous act has its tutelary angel, and they worshiped this angel as they abandoned themselves to incredible debauches.

'Ewen, an ancient king of England, had established by law in his counties that no girl could marry unless he had taken her virginity. In the whole of Scotland, and in parts of France, the powerful lords enjoyed this right.

'Women, as well as men, arrive at cruelty through license. Three hundred women of Inca Atabaliba, in Peru, prostituted themselves at once to the Spaniards, and aided them in the massacre of their husbands.

'Sodomy is general throughout the earth; there is no people that does not practice it; not a great man but is given to it. The cult of Sappho shares this reign. This passion belongs to Nature just as the other one does; it forms in the heart of a girl, at the tenderest age, at the age of candor and innocence, when she has received no alien impression; then, she is the voice of Nature, then, she is stamped with Nature's hand.

'Bestiality was universal. Xenophon tells us that during the retreat of the Ten Thousand, the Greeks made use only of goats. This practice is widespread throughout Italy to this day; *le bou cest meilleur que sa femmelle; son anus, plus étroit, est plus chaud; et cet animal, naturellement lubrique, s'agite de lui-même dès qu'il s'aperçoit qu'on décharge: sois bien persuadée, Juliette, que je n'en parle que par expérience.*

'*Le dindon est délicieux, mais il faut lui couper le cou à l'instant*

124

de la crise; le resserrement de son boyau vous comble alors de volupté.[1]

'The Sybarites were bestial with dogs; Egyptian women prostituted themselves to crocodiles; American women to baboons. In the end they turned to statues; everybody knows that one of Louis XV's page-boys was found discharging over the backside of the Venus Callipyge. A Greek who came to Delphos to consult the oracle found two marble genii in the temple, and in the night did lustful homage to the one he found more handsome. When all was done he crowned him with laurel, a reward for the pleasures he had received of him.

'The Siamese not only believe suicide permissible, but they go so far as to think that killing oneself is a sacrifice profitable to the soul, and that this sacrifice assures its happiness in the next world.

'In Pegu, for five days on end they turn and re-turn over burning coals the woman who has just given birth; thus she is purified.

'The Caribbeans purchase children from the very breast of the mother; they dye the bellies of these children with roucou the day they are born, take their virginity when they are seven or eight, and generally kill them after they have served their purpose.

'In the island of Nicaragua, a father is allowed to sell his children for *immolation;* and when these people consecrate their maize, they sprinkle it with sperm, and dance around this twin product of nature.

'In Brazil, a woman is awarded to every prisoner who is to be sacrificed; he enjoys her; and the woman, often pregnant by him, helps to cut him to shreds and takes part in the meal that is made of his flesh.

'Before being ruled by the Incas, the ancient inhabitants of Peru (that is to say the first pioneers who came from Scythia, those who were the first to people America) had a custom of sacrificing their children to their gods.

'The peoples from round about Rio Réal substituted for the circumcision of their daughters – a ceremony customary in a number of nations – a strange enough practice; as soon as they have reached marriageable age, they thrust into their wombs sticks crawling with huge ants which sting them horribly; they take care to renew these sticks to prolong the agony, which never lasts for less than three months and sometimes considerably longer.

[1] *On en trouve dans plusieurs bordels de Paris; la fille alors lui passe la tête entre les cuisses, vous avez son cul pour perspective, et elle coupe le cou de l'animal au moment de votre décharge: nous verrons peut-être beintot cette fantaisie en action.*

'Saint Jerome recounts that, during a journey he made among the Gauls, he saw Scotchmen eating, with extreme pleasure, the buttocks of shepherd lads and the breasts of maidens. I would rather trust to the first of these dishes than to the second; and in company with all cannibal tribes, I believe that the flesh of women, as the flesh of all female animals, is necessarily very inferior to that of the male species.

'The Mingrelians and the Georgians are the handsomest people on earth and at the same time the most addicted to every variety of indulgence and crime, as if Nature had wished to apprise us in this way that these deviations offend her so little that she wishes to accord all these gifts to those most partial to them. Incest, rape, infanticide, prostitution, adultery, murder, theft, sodomy, lesbianism, bestiality, burning, poisoning, abduction, parricide – to them these are virtuous acts to be proud of. Whenever they come together, it is simply to exchange talk of the immensity or enormity of their crimes; reminiscences or plans for such acts become the core of their most delectable conversations; thus they stir themselves to commit new crimes.

'To the north of Tartary there is a people that creates a new god for itself every day; this god has to be the first object encountered on waking in the morning. If by chance it is a turd, a turd is the idol of the day; and by hypothesis, is this not as worthy as the ridiculous god of flour worshiped by the Catholics? One is already excremental matter, and the other will soon be; in truth, the difference is very slight.

'In the province of Matomba, they shut children of both sexes in a very dark house when they reach the age of twelve; here they undergo, by way of initiation, every ill-treatment it pleases the priests to impose upon them, without these children being able to reveal anything or to complain when they leave such houses.

'When a girl is married in Ceylon, it is her brothers who take her maidenhead; her husband never has a right to it.

'We consider pity as a feeling that will bring us to do good works; in Kamchatka it is more logically considered a fault. Among this people it would be held a cardinal vice to withdraw someone from the danger into which fate has flung him. If these people see a man drowning, they pass by without stopping, and they are very careful not to give him any help.

'Forgiving one's enemies is a virtue among the idiot Christians; in Brazil, it is a magnificent deed to kill and eat them.

'In Guiana they expose a girl naked to the biting of flies the first time she menstruates; frequently she dies in the process.

126

The delighted spectator on this occasion spends the whole day in exhilaration.

'On the wedding eve of a young woman in Brazil, they make a large number of wounds in her buttocks, so that her husband, already moved by the blood and the climate to revulsion from the physical, will at last be repulsed by the branding set before him.

'The few examples I have collected will be sufficient to show you, Juliette, what those virtues our European laws and religions make so much of really are, what this odious thread of brotherhood, so praised by unspeakable Christianity, is. You can see whether it is or is not in the human heart; would so many execrations be so widespread, if the existence of the virtue they opposed had any reality?

'I will never cease to repeat to you: this feeling for humanity is a fantasy; it can never belong to the passions, nor even to the needs, for in sieges men are seen to devour each other. It is then no more than a feeling of weakness absolutely alien to Nature, an offspring of fear and prejudice. Can we hide from ourselves the fact that Nature gives us our needs and our passions? Yet needs and passions are unmindful of the virtue of humanity; therefore that virtue is not in Nature; and thence it is purely an effect of the egoism that has brought us to desire peace with our kind, in order to enjoy it ourselves. But the man who does not fear retaliation binds himself only with the greatest of difficulty to a duty respectable only to those who are apprehensive of retaliation. Ah, no, no, Juliette, there is no unadulterated pity, no pity which does not turn back on ourselves. Let us analyze ourselves thoroughly at the moment when we catch ourselves commiserating, and we shall see that deep in our hearts a hidden voice cries: *You weep over this wretch because you are wretched yourself and you fear you will become more so*. Now what is that voice but the voice of fear? And where is fear born but in egoism?'

2

'My brothers,' said [Belmor], 'I have promised to speak to the society today on love; and although this discourse may appear to be addressed only to the men, the women, I assure you, will learn as well all that is necessary to preserve them from so dangerous a sentiment. . . .

'Love is the name we give to the inner feeling that draws us, so to speak, in spite of ourselves, towards some object that imparts to us a sharp desire to unite with it, to come close to it time and time again, an object that delights us, that intoxicates us when we achieve that union, and that reduces us to despair and tears us with anguish, when some extraneous cause obliges us to break this union. If this extravagance never did more than lead us to ardent, intoxicated possession, it would only be an absurdity; but since it leads us to a certain metaphysic that, by transforming us into the thing loved, makes its acts, wants, and desires as dear to us as our very own, by this alone it becoms excessively dangerous for it takes us out of ourselves too much, and causes us to neglect our own interests for those of the thing loved. Identifying us, so to speak, with this thing, we are made to adopt its miseries and vexations and to add them to the sum ot ours. What is more, the fear either of losing this object, or of seeing it grow cold, plagues us incessantly, and from a most peaceable state in our life we pass insensibly, by accepting this fetter, to doubtless the cruelest one that can be imagined in the world. If the compensation or indemnity for so many pains were other than ordinary enjoyment, perhaps I would advise risking it; but all the cares, the torments, the thorns of love never lead to anything that cannot easily be obtained without it. Where, then, is the need for its irons?

'When a beautiful woman submits to me and I fall in love with her, I have no object different from that of the man who sees her and desires her without formulating any kind of love. We both wish to sleep with her; *he* only wants her body; *I*, by false and dangerous metaphysics that blind me to my real motive, which is that of my rival, persuade myself that it is only her heart that I want, that any notion of enjoyment is out of the question. I persuade myself so well that I should be only too willing to agree to love this woman for herself, and to purchase her heart at the price of sacrificing all my physical desires.

'Here is the grievous cause of my folly; here is what will drag me into that fearful abyss of affliction; here is what will blight my life; in that moment all will be changed – suspicions, jealousies, fears, will become the bitter nourishment of my unfortunate existence. The nearer I get to my happiness, the more certain it will be, and the inevitable fear of losing it will poison my days so much the more.

'By renouncing the thorns of this dangerous feeling, do not imagine that I deny myself its roses. Then I should pluck them securely, I should have the best of the flower, scattering all that was incongruous; likewise I should possess the body I desire, but not the soul that is of no use to me. If man were more enlightened as to his real interests in sensual enjoyment, he would spare his heart the cruel fever that burns and parches it. If he were able to convince himself that there is no need whatsoever to be loved in order to enjoy thoroughly, and that love rather detracts from the ecstasies of pleasure than adds to them, he would renounce these metaphysics of feeling that blind him, would confine himself to simple bodily enjoyment, and would know true happiness, forever sparing himself the grief inseparable from its dangerous scruples.

'This refinement that we locate in the desire to enjoy is an imaginary, quite chimerical feeling, of some value perhaps in the metaphysics of love; but then that is the case with all illusions – they flourish reciprocally. Yet this feeling is useless, and even harmful, in matters that relate simply to the satisfaction of the senses. From this moment, as you see, love becomes completely useless; and the man of reason may no longer see in the object of his enjoyment anything but an object for which his nervous fluid is set ablaze, a creature extremely indifferent in herself, who gives herself up to the purely physical satisfaction of the desires kindled by her in this fluid, and who, once this satisfaction is given and taken, returns, in the eyes of the man of reason, to the category she previously occupied.

'She is not the only one of her kind; he can find others as willing and as good. He lived well before meeting her; why should he not live in like fashion afterwards? How could the infidelity of this woman disturb him, whatever form it took? Does she deprive her lover of anything by lavishing her favors on another? He had his turn, so what has he to complain of? Why should another not have her as well? And what does he lose in this creature that he may not find at once in another? Besides, if she deceives him for a rival, she may just as well deceive this rival for him; this second lover will then be no more loved than the first; why, if this is so, should he be jealous, since neither the one nor the other is the better treated? These sorrows would be pardonable, at the very most, if this beloved woman were unique in the world; the moment the loss is reparable, they become extravagances.

'To put myself for a moment in the position of the first lover, what, I ask you, does this creature possess to occasion me such pain? A little attention to my person, some reciprocation of my feelings; illusion alone endowed them with power, and it was the desire to possess this woman, it was interest that adorned her in my eyes, it was – either because I had not had enough pleasure, or through some residue of my early mistakes – that the veil I was accustomed to wear before enjoyment fell about my eyes again, and in spite of myself. And I do not tear it away! Weakness . . . pusillanimity! Let us evaluate this goddess after taking pleasure, this goddess who blinded me before. . . .

'Let us use this period of calm and exhaustion to consider her in cold blood, to spend a moment, as Lucretius says, behind the scenes of life. Well then, we see this object that turns our head, we see it with the same desires, the same needs, the same bodily form, the same appetites . . . afflicted with the same infirmities as all the other creatures of its sex, and ridding ourselves in this cold-blooded examination of the ridiculous enthusiasm that drew us towards this object, similar in every detail to all others of its kind, we see that without it we lose nothing that we cannot easily replace. . . .

'Let us go so far as to say this: in no case is woman formed for man's exclusive happiness. From the point of view of enjoyment, she certainly does not completely supply him, since man finds a keener enjoyment with his own kind. As a friend, her duplicity, her submissiveness, or rather her lowness, are opposed to the perfection of the sense of friendship. Friendship demands candor and equality; if one of two friends dominates the other, friendship is destroyed. Now, this authority of one of the two sexes over the other fatal though it is to friendship, necessarily exists between two friends of different sex; a woman, then, is neither good as mistress nor as friend, Her only real position is in the slavery the Orientals keep her in; she is good only for enjoyment, beyond which, as good King Chiperic said, you must pull out as quickly as possible.

'If it is easily proved that love is only a national prejudice, that three-quarters of the peoples of the world who habitually cloister their women have never known this frenzy of the imagination, then by going back to the source of this prejudice we may readily assure ourselves that it is nothing more, and so arrive at a means of curing it. Now it is certain, as I say, that this turn of mind derives from the age-old respect our ancestors had for women, by reason of the role of prophetess they exercised in towns and in the country; fear led from respect to a cult, and gallantry was born in the heart of superstition. But this respect was never present in Nature, and it would be a waste of time to look for it there. The inferiority of this sex to our own is too well established ever to stimulate in us any real motive for respecting it; and love, which is born of this blind respect, is simply a prejudice. Respect for women increases as the spirit of government moves further away from the principles of Nature; so long as men obey these first laws, they may royally disdain women. When men are debased, women become gods; for it follows necessarily that when men grow weak, the weaker must govern as the stronger are degraded; government is always infirm when women reign. But do not quote Turkey at me; if her government is weak, it is only since plots in the seraglio have curbed its progress. The Turks destroyed the empire of Constantinople when they trailed this sex in chains and when, in full view of the army, Mahomet severed Irene's head, Irene who was suspected of having too great an influence on him. There is meanness and depravity in avowing the slightest worship of women; even in drunkenness it is an impossible cult, and what else can be suspected afterwards? If the usefulness of a thing becomes a reason for worshiping it, you must equally worship your ox, your ass, your chamber pot, and so on.

'In a word, what is called love is nothing else but the desire to enjoy; so long as it lasts, worship is pointless; and as soon as it is satisfied, it is impossible. Which goes to prove most certainly that respect did not arise from worship, but rather worship from respect. Cast your eyes back to those examples of the degradation in which this sex was held formerly, and where it still is among a large proportion of peoples, and you will at last be convinced that the metaphysical passion of love is by no means innate in man, that it is the fruit of his prejudices and customs, and that the object which gave rise to this generally despised passion should never have blinded him. . . .

'Infidelity and libertinage: there, my friends, are the two anti-dotes to love. . . . By force of habit, the heart insensibly loses that dangerous softness that makes it liable to impressions of love; it turns indifferent, hardens, and the cure soon follows. Why should I tremble at the severities of this insolent creature when, if I thought a little, I should see that a couple of louis can procure me a body as beautiful as hers, and with no difficulty?

'Let us never lose sight of the fact that the woman who most tries to charm us in is certainly concealing faults that would most certainly disgust us if we did but know them. Let us imagine them, suspect them, guess at them – these details; and this first process, at the very moment love is born, will perhaps extinguish it. If she is a maiden, be assured she will reek of some unhealthy odor, if not at one period, then at another: is it really worth while going going into raptures over a cloaca? If she is a woman, the traces of some other man may, I do agree, arouse desires for a moment – but our love? And what is there to be worshiped there . . . the caver-nous mold of a dozen children. Put yourself in mind of her, this divinity of your heart, as she is giving birth; look at this shapeless mass of flesh coming out foul and viscous from the center where you think to find happiness; and last, undress the idol of your soul, at any time – are these the short and crooked thighs that turn your head? Or the fetid, infected pit that they support? Or perhaps her

131

crumpled apron, falling in folds about these same thighs, will heat your imagination? Or those two flacid globes hanging down to the navel?

'But perhaps you pay homage to the reverse of the medal. And these are two pieces of flabby, yellowish flesh closing over a ghastly hole that joins on the other. Oh! yes, these are certainly the attractions your mind feasts on! And it is to enjoy them that you set yourselves below the most stupid of beasts! But I am mistaken; none of this attracts you. You are snared by very much finer qualities. It is that treacherous, double character, that everlasting state of lying and deceit, that shrewish tone, that voice that sounds like a cat's, that sluttishness or prudery – for no woman escapes one of these two extremes – that slander . . . that wickedness . . . that contradiction . . . that irrelevance. . . . Yes, yes, I do see how binding these attractions are, and without a doubt their turning your head is well worth the trouble . . .

'But I daresay someone will object that their adoration always existed; the Greeks and the Romans made gods of Love and his mother. To that I reply that this worship must have had the same principle as ours; among the Greeks and Romans women predicted the future too, and from this was born respect and the cult of respect. . . . In any case, not much reliance is to be placed on Greeks and Romans as to objects of worship; the people who adored excrement under the name of the god Stercutious and the sewers under that of the goddess Cloacina may well have worshiped women, so often linked by smell to these ancient divinities.

'So, then, let us be wise to the end, and treat these ridiculous idols as the Japanese treat theirs when they do not get what they want. Worship, or appear to worship if you will, until what is desired is obtained; and despise them as soon as you gain it. If you are refused, give the idol a hundred blows with a stick, to teach it not to disdain your wishes; or if you prefer, imitate the Ostians who thrash their gods with all their might the moment they are dissatisfied. The worthless God must be smashed. . . .

'Love is a physical need; beware of ever thinking of it otherwise. "Love," says Voltaire, "is the fabric of Nature embroidered by the imagination." The aim of love, of its desires and pleasures – all is physical. Never go near the thing that might seem something more than that. Absence and variety are sure remedies for love; you soon forget the one you have stopped seeing, and new pleasures consume the memory of the old. Remorse for loss is soon forgotten. Those pleasures that are irrecoverable may cause bitter regrets, but those that are readily replaced, those that are born minute by minute, at every street corner, should not cost us a tear.'

3

[Juliette, who tells the story, is traveling in Italy with her friends. One day, in Lombardy, as they are viewing a volcano, they are addressed by a giant, seven feet and three inches tall, wearing enormous twisted-up mustaches, and with a face as dark as the devil's. His name is Minski, and he invites them to visit his castle where he promises to show them some 'astonishing things.' They accept, and their host leads the way.]

Leaving the volcanic plain of Pietra-Mala, we spent an hour climbing a high mountain lying to the right. From the peak of this mountain we caught sight of abysses more than two thousand fathoms deep, and to these we directed our steps. All that region was shrouded in woods so clustered so prodigiously thick, that we could scarcely see our way through. After a sheer descent lasting nearly three hours, we reached the shores of a vast lake. On an island in the middle of that water was to be seen the stronghold that was our guide's lair; the height of the outer walls surrounding it was the reason for our only being able to make out the roof. For six hours we had walked without coming across a habitation of any kind. . . . We saw no one.

A ferry, black like the Venetian gondolas, awaited us at the edge of the lake. It was from here that we were able to survey the fearful hollow we were in; on all sides it was surrounded by mountains as far as the eye could see, and their summits and barren sides were covered with fir, larch, and ilex. No more dismal and uncouth sight could have met the eye; you would have thought it the edge of the world. We stepped into the ferry; the giant steered it single-handed. From the haven to the castle was still three hundred fathoms. We arrived at the foot of an iron gate cut into the solid wall that ran round the castle; here we encountered moats ten feet across, and crossed them by a bridge that lifted as soon as we had passed. A second wall appeared, again we went through an iron gate, and we found ourselves in a woody mass so compact that we thought it impossible to proceed farther. In truth we could go no farther, because the mass, formed of a quickset hedge, offered only sharp points. In its heart was the château's last *enceinte*, ten feet thick. The giant lifted a stone of enormous size that he alone could grapple. A winding staircase was revealed; the stone closed to, and by way of the bowels of the earth, ever in shadows, we reached the center vaults of the house, from which we ascended by means of an opening guarded by a stone similar to the one just mentioned. So here we were, in a low room entirely lined with skeletons; the seats in this place were constructed only of the bones of the dead; and whether one liked it or not, one sat down on skulls. Fearful cries seemed to us to emanate from below ground, and we quickly learned that the dungeons where this monster's victims groaned were situated in the vaults of this room.

When we were seated, Minski said to us, 'You are in my power: I can do with you what I please. However, don't be frightened; the actions I have seen you commit are so close to my way of thinking that I believed you worthy of knowing and partaking of the pleasures of my retreat. Listen to me; I have time to instruct you before supper, which will be prepared while I talk to you.

'I am a Muscovite, born in a village on the banks of the Volga. My name is Minski. When my father died he left me immense riches, and Nature shaped my physical faculties and tastes to meet those favors Fortune bestowed upon me. Feeling myself in no wise made to vegetate deep in an obscure province like that in which I had first seen the light of day, I traveled. The whole universe did not seem vast enough for the span of my desires; it offered me limits, and I wanted none. A born libertine, impious, debauched, bloody, and ferocious, I roved the world only in order to learn its vices, and acquired them only to refine upon them. I began with China, the kingdom of the Great Mogul, and Tartary; I went over all Asia; proceeding to Kamchatka, I entered America by the famous Bering Strait. I passed through that vast quarter of the world, now with civilized peoples, now with savages, and never imitating anything but the crimes of the one lot, and the vices and atrocities of the other. So dangerous were the tendencies I brought back to your Europe that I was condemned to be burned in Spain, broken in France, hanged in England, and clubbed to death in Italy. My wealth protected me against all that.

'I went to Africa, and it was there that I fully realized that what you are so foolish as to call depravation is never anything but the natural state of man, and more frequently the result of the soil Nature has thrown him on. These hardy children of the sun laughed at me when I wanted to reproach them with their babarity towards their wives. "And what," they replied, "is a wife unless the domestic animal Nature provides us with to satisfy both our needs and our pleasures? What rights has she to deserve more from us than our farmyard beasts do? The only difference we see in it," these judicious peoples told me, 'is that our domestic animals may deserve some indulgence by reason of their meekness and submission, while the women deserve only severity and barbarity for their perpetual state of deceit, naughtiness, betrayal, and perfidy. And then we sleep with them too, and what better can you do with a woman you have slept with than treat her like an ox or an ass, or slaughter her for food?"

'In a word, it was there that I observed man vicious by temperament, cruel by instinct, ferocious by education; this disposition pleased me; I found it more akin to Nature; and I liked it more than the American's unadorned vulgarity, than the European's imposture, than the Asiatic's shameless sensuality. Having hunted men to death with the first, drunk and lied with the second, and fornicated with the third, I now ate human beings with these others. I have retained this taste; all the debris of bodies you see here is simply the remains of creatures I eat; I only feed on human flesh; and I hope you will be pleased with the feast of it I propose to have prepared for you. A boy of fifteen I had yesterday has been killed for our supper, he should be delicious.

'After ten years of travel, I returned to make a tour of my homeland. My mother and my sister were still alive. I was natural heir to both of them. Not wishing to set foot in Muscovy again, I considered it vital to my interests to reconcile these two successions I ravished and murdered them both on the same day. My mother still retained her beauty, and was as tall as myself; and my sister, although only six feet tall, was the most superb creature to be seen in the two Russias.

'I gathered all that could come to me from these inheritances; and finding I had something like two millions to squander every year, I returned to Italy with the intention of settling there. But I wanted an unusual, mysterous situation in the wilds, where I could abandon myself to all the treacherous waywardness of my imagination; and such deviations are no trifling matters, my friends, as I hope you will see, however few days we spend together. There is no single dissolute passion that is not dear to my heart, not a crime that has not beguiled me. If I have not committed more crimes than I have, it has been for want of occasion; I cannot reproach myself with having neglected a single opportunity; and I have forced those [situations] that were not coming to a head with sufficient energy. If I had been so fortunate as to have doubled the sum of my crimes, I should have had all the happier memories of them; for memories of crime are delights that cannot be overincreased.

'This aim will make me appear a villain in your sight, and I hope that what you will witness in this house will confirm this reputation to me. Have no doubts as to the extent of these acommodations; it is immense, *et renferme deux cents petits garçons, dans l'âge de cinq à seize ans, qui passent communément de mon lit dans ma boucherie, et à peu près le même nombre de jeunes gens*

135

*destinés à me foutre. J'aime infiniment cette sensation; il n'en est
pas de plus douce au monde que celle d'avoir le cul vigoureusement
limé, pendant qu'on s'amuse soi-meme de telle manière que ce
puisse être. Les plaisirs que je vous ai vus goûter tantôt sur le bord du
volcan me prouvent que vous partagez cette façon de perdre du
foutre, et voilà pourquoi je vous parle avec autant de franchise; je
ferais, sans cela, tout simplement de vous des victimes.*

'I keep two harems. The first comprises two hundred girls
aged from five to twenty, whom I eat when, by dint of lechery,
they are sufficiently mortified. Two hundred women aged from
twenty to thirty are in the second, and you shall see how I treat
them. Fifty valets of both sexes are employed in the service of this
considerable number of objects of lust; and to recruit them, I have
a hundred women agents dispersed through the cities of the world.
Would you believe that with the colossal coming and going all
this demands, there is nevertheless only the one way of entering
my island, the way you have just come? There should be no doubt,
certainly, as to the quantity of creatures who tread this mysterious path.

'The veils I draw over all this will never be torn apart. Not that
I have the slightest thing to fear; this place is part of the States
of the Grand Duke of Tuscany; they know everything about the
irregularity of my conduct; and the money I spread about shelters
me from everything.

'And now for you to make my complete acquaintance, you
must have a little more about myself. I am forty-five, my lecherous
talents are such *que je ne me couche jamais sans avoir déchargé dix
fois. Il est vrai que l'extrême quantité de chair humaine dont je me
nourris contribue beacoup à l'augmentation et à l'épaisseur de la
matière séminale.* Whoever tries this regime will certainly multiply
his libidinous abilities threefold, quite apart from the strength,
health, and freshness this food will maintain in him. I am not
speaking of his pleasure: suffice it for you to know that once it
has been tasted, it is no longer possible to eat anything else, and
that there is not a single meat, animal, or fish, that can compare. It
is only a matter of getting over the first revulsions; and once the
barriers are down, you can never have enough. *Comme j'espère que
nous déchargerons ensemble, il est essentiel que je vous prévienne des
effrayants symptômes de cette crise en moi; d'epouvantables
hurlements la précèdent, l'accompagnent, et les jets du sperme
élancés pour lors s'élèvent au plancher, souvent dans le nombre de
quinze ou vingt: jamais la multiplicité des plaisirs ne m'épuise; mes
éjaculations sont aussi tumultueuses, aussi abontantes à la diex-
ième fois qu'à la première, et je ne me suis jamais senti le lendemain*

des fatigues de la veille; à l'égard du membre dont tout cela part, le voici, dit Minski, en mettant au jour un anchois, de dix-huit pouces de long, sur seize de circonférence, surmonté d'un champignon vermeil et large comme de cul d'un chapeau. Oui, le voici: il est toujours dans l'état où le vous le voyez, meme en dormant, meme en marchant.'

'Mais, mon cher hôte, vous tuez donc autant de femmes et de garçons que vous en voyez.'

'Almost,' replied the Muscovite, *'et comme je mange ce que je fouts, cela m'évite la peine d'avoir un boucher.* You need a great deal of wisdom to understand me, I realize. I am a monster, spewed up by Nature to assist her in the destructions she demands. I am a being unique to my species . . . a . . . Oh, yes I know all the invectives conferred upon me, yet strong enough not to need anyone, wise enough to be satisfied in my solitude, to detest all men, to brave their censure, and to care nothing for their opinion of me, learned enough to crush all cults, to flout all religions, and to give not a damn for all the gods, proud enough to abhor all governments, to put myself above all ties, restraints, moral principles; I am happy in my little kingdom. Here I exercise every sovereign right. I taste all the pleasures of despotism, I fear no man, and I live contented. I make few visits, none, even, unless in my walks I come across beings like yourselves who appear to me philosophical enough to come and entertain themselves for a time in my place; these are the only people I invite, and I meet few of them. The powers Nature has endowed me with make me stretch these walks very far; never a day but I do twelve of fifteen leagues. . . . '

'And consequently make a few captures,' I broke in.

'Captures, thefts, fires, murders, every criminal possibility presented to me, I commit. because Nature has given me the taste and ability for all crimes, and there is not one that is not dear to me, and from which I do not derive the fondest pleasures.'

'And justice?'

'It is nowhere in this land. That is why I have set myself here; with money you can do all you want – and I circulate a great deal of it.'

Two of Minski's male slaves, swarthy and repulsive, came to announce that supper was ready. They fall on their knees before their master, *lui baisèrent respectueusement les couiles et le trou du cul* – and we passed into another room.

'There are no special preparations for you,' said the giant. 'All the kings on earth might come visiting me, but I would not deviate from my habits.'

Yet the place and the properties of the room are worth describing.

'The furniture you see here,' our host told us, 'is alive. It will move at a mere sign.'

Minski made this sign, and the table came forward. From a corner of the room, it took up a position in the middle; similarly, five armchairs spaced themselves about it, two chandeliers came down from the ceiling and overhung the center of the table.

'An elementary mechanism,' said the giant making us look closer at the substance of this furniture. 'You will notice that this table, these chandeliers, and chairs are simply made up of groups of girls, artistically arranged. My dishes will be laid, hot as they are, on the backs of these creatures; *mes bougies sont enforcées dans leurs cons; et mon derrière, ainsi que les vôtres, en se nichant dans ses fauteuils, vont être appuyés sur les doux visages ou les blancs tétons de ces demoiselles; c'est pour cela que je vous prie de vous trousser, mesdames, et vous, messieurs, de vous déculotter, afin que, d'après les paroles de l'écriture, "la chair puisse se reposer sur la chair." '*

'Minski,' I pointed out to our Muscovite, 'the girls' role is wearying, especially if you are too long at table.'

'The very worst that can happen,' said Minski, 'is that some of them die, and these losses are too easily replaced for me to bother my head over it for a moment.'

Au moment où nous nous troussions, et où les hommes se déculottaient, Minski exigea que nos fesses lui fussent présentées; il les mania, il les mordit, et nous remarquâmes que, de nos quatre culs, celui de Sbrigani, par un raffinement de caprices facile à supposer dans un tel homme, fut celui qu'il fêta le plus; il le gamahucha pendant près d'un quart d'heure; cette cérémonie faite, nous nous assîmes à cru sur les tétons et les visages des sultanes, ou plutôt des esclaves de Minski.

A dozen naked girls, between twenty and twenty-five years old, served the dishes on to the living tables, and since they were of silver and extremely hot, by burning the buttocks or nipples of the creatures who composed these tables, there resulted a most pleasant compulsive motion, like the swelling of the sea. More than twenty entrées or roasts embellished the table; and on sideboards made of girls in groups of four, who likewise came up at the slightest signal, were laid wines of every kind.

'My friends,' said our host, 'I warned you that only human flesh is eaten here; none of the dishes you see here but is made of that.'

'We will try it,' said Sbrigani. 'Revulsions are absurdities; they arise only in defect of habit. All meats are made to nourish man, all are offered us to this end by Nature, and it is no more extraordinary to eat a man than a chicken.'

With these words, my husband plunged his fork into a gammon of boy that seemed to him to be done to a turn, and after helping at least two pounds onto his plate, he ate it. I followed suit. Minski encouraged us; and as his appetite was the size of his passion, he had soon cleared a dozen dishes.

Minski drank as he ate; he was already on his thirtieth bottle of Burgundy when they served the second course, which he washed down with champagne. Aleatico, Falernian, and other rare Italian wines were drunk at dessert.

More than thirty more bottles had made their way to the guts of our anthropophage when, his senses sufficiently heightened by all this physical and moral rioting, the brute announced to us that he wanted to unload.

'I won't have any of your four,' he said, 'because it would kill you, but at least you can assist my pleasures ... you shall scrutinize them; I hold you worthy to be excited by them. . . . Well then, whom do you want me to have?'

'I wish,' I said to Minski, who was leaning lustfully over me and seemed very desirous of me, 'I wish you to. . . .'

*   *   *

'*Eh quoi! dis-je aussitôt qu'il eut déchargé une seconde fois, vous ne goûtez donc jamais ce plaisir qu'il n'en coûte la vie à un individu?*'
'*Au moins, répond l'ogre, il faut qu'une créature humaine meure pendant que je fous; je ne déchargerais pas sans l'alliance des soupirs de la mort à ceux de ma lubricité, et je ne dois jamais l'éjaculation de mon foutre qu'à l'idée cette mort que j'occasionne.*

'But let us go into another room,' the anthropophage went on, 'Ices, coffee, and liqueurs await us. . . .'

We went in. From the prevailing odor of the place, we readily guessed the kind of ices that were offered us. In five bowls of white porcelain, there were set a dozen of fifteen *étrons* of the most elegant shape, and very newly laid.

'Here are the ices,' the ogre told us, 'that I consume after dinner. Nothing is so good for the digestion, and at the same time, nothing gives me so much pleasure. These *étrons* come from the best seats in my seraglio, and you may eat them with every confidence.'

'Minski,' I replied, 'a great deal of practice is necessary for that dish; we might perhaps take to it in a moment of aberration, but in cold blood, never.'

'Exactly so,' said the ogre, taking hold of a bowl and swallowing the contents, 'do just as you wish, you are under no constraint from me. Here, there are liqueurs; I will have mine afterwards.'

139

Nothing was so baleful as the lighting of this room, and it was in perfect harmony with the rest. Twenty-four death's-heads enclosed a lamp whose beams shot through the eyes and jaws. I had never seen anything so frightening.

* * *

At eleven o'clock, Minski sent word to us that we would be accorded the honor of visiting him in his bed. We entered; his bedroom was very large; and we saw there superb frescoes representing ten licentious tableaux whose composition could well pass for the *nec plus ultra* of lewdness.

At the end of this room was a huge alcove encircled with mirrors and ornamented with sixteen pillars of black marble, to each of which was bound a young girl, her back being visible. By means of two cords placed, like bell ropes, at our hero's bed head, he could have a different torture fall on each of the backsides pointed at him, and which lasted as long as the cord was not pulled a second time. . . . He asked us if we would like to see the way in which he could simultaneously injure the sixteen girls tied to the pillars. I urged him to show us this strange contrivance. He pulled on these fatal ropes and, as they all cried out together, these sixteen wretched creatures sustained a different wound apiece. These found themselves pricked, burned, flagellated; those, torn with pincers, cut, clipped, scratched, and all with such vehemence that blood flowed from every part.

'If I redoubled the effect,' said Minski, 'and that does sometimes happen, *selon l'état de mes couilles,* as I was saying, if I redoubled my efforts, these sixteen whores would perish in my sight at one and the same blow. I love to fall asleep toying with the notion of being able to commit sixteen murders at once, at my slightest whim.'

[During the course of an orgy, Minski kills one of Juliette's companions. This, together with their other frightening experiences in the castle of the ogre, makes Juliette and her friends resolve to attempt to get out alive. They feed Minski some chocolate into which they have put a sleeping potion; and when he falls asleep, they take as much of his treasure as they can carry and make good their escape.]

4

Conversation became general, and was soon enlivened by philosophy. Albani showed us a letter from Bologna, in which he was informed of the death of one of his friends, who, although highly placed in the Church, had always lived licentiously, and even in his last moments had not wished to be converted.

'You knew him,' he said to Bernis, 'there was never any preaching to him. He kept his head and his fine wit to the last, and died in the arms of a niece he adored, assuring her that what vexed him in being constrained to deny the existence of heaven was the despair it left him in, the despair of not meeting her again one day.'

'It seems to me,' said the Cardinal de Bernis, 'that such deaths are becoming frequent; the author of *Alzire* and d'Alembert have made them fashionable.'

'To be sure,' said Albani, 'there is considerable weakness in changing your mind on your deathbed. Have we not time to make up our minds in the course of so long a life? The years of vigor and vitality should be used in choosing some system or other, and living and dying by it once it has been adopted. To be still uncertain at this age is to bring upon oneself a fearful death. Perhaps you will tell me that the crisis deranges the organs and so weakens that system. That is so, if such systems are embraced newly or lightly, but never when they are stamped on the mind early in life, when they have been the fruits of labor, study, and reflection, because then they form habits, and habits do not leave us in our lifetime.'

'To be sure,' I [Juliette] replied, flattered with being able to impart my way of thinking to the famous libertines in whose presence I found myself, 'and if contented stoicism, to which I, like you, adhere deprives us of a few pleasures, it spares us many pains, and teaches us how to die. I do not know,' I went on, 'whether it is because I am only twenty-five and that time that should return me to the elements I am formed of is perhaps still far-off, or whether it is really my principles that sustain and encourage me, but I view the disintegration of the particles of my existence without any fear. Most firmly decided not to be more unhappy after life than I was before being born, it seems that I am returning my body to the earth, as calmly and indifferently as I received it.'

'And what gives rise to such peace in you?' said Bernis. 'It is the deep distrust you have always had for religious mummery. A single backward step towards it and you would have been lost. You can never be too soon in trampling it underfoot.'

'Is that as easy as is thought?' asked Olympe.

'It is easy,' said Albani. 'But the tree must be cut from the root. If you merely labor to remove the branches, buds will always be growing.'

5

'I have nothing to fear,' said the Count. 'I operate from the heights of a hill in the center of Rome. The thirty-seven invisible bombs that I aim at the thirty-seven hospitals shall be repeated, and such are my methods that no one will see them. I shall project them at intervals so that fire will be spread by the very means used to extinguish it, and fire will always break out in proportion to the precautions taken to soak it up.'

'You would set a whole town aflame, Count,' asked Olympe, 'by these terrible methods?'

'Indeed,' answered the doctor, 'and very likely half the town will perish simply by what we are doing. Ghigi says there are hospitals situated in the poorest quarters of Rome, and these parts will most assuredly perish.'

'Do such considerations stop you?' asked Olympe.

'Not in the least, madame,' the two instigators of this atrocity replied together.

'The gentlemen seem quite inflexible,' I said to Madame de Borghèse. 'I believe they have thought it over, and the crime they are going to commit is but a very mild thing to them.'

'There is no crime in what we plan,' said Ghigi. 'All our moral blunders arise from the unreasonableness of our ideas on good and evil.

'If we were convinced of the neutrality of all our acts, if we really believed that those we call right are no less than that in the eyes of Nature, and that those we call inquitious are perhaps, by her lights, the most perfect standard of reason and equity, then surely we would make far fewer miscalculations. But childhood prejudices deceive us, and will never stop leading us into error so long as we are weak enough to listen to them. It seems that the torch of reason only lights our way when we are no longer able to profit from its beams, and that it is only after folly on folly that we come to discover the source of all those follies ignorance has caused us to commit.'

6

All three of us were seated in Faustine's grave, and Olympe spoke to us in somewhat this manner:

'My friends, there are two things that I have never understood,' this lively and lovable woman said, 'reverence for the dead, and respect for their wishes. There is no doubt that both of these are due to current conceptions of the immortality of the soul; for if people were thoroughly convinced of the principles of materialism, if they truly believed that we are only a sorry compound of material elements, and that once struck by death, dissolution is complete, then the homage paid to these disorganized scraps of matter would certainly be so palpable an absurdity that no one would wish to make it. But our pride will not bend to the certainty of ceasing to exist. We believe the shades of the dead still hover about their corpses and are sensible of devotions made to these hulks; we fear to offend them, and so fall imperceptibly into impiety and absurdity in the extreme. Let us then be certain of the scheme of things in which absolutely nothing more of us exists when we are dead, and the remains we leave on earth are no more than our excrement was when we laid it at the foot of a tree. Full of this scheme, we would feel that no respect or obligation was due to a corpse, and that the only attention it deserved was to be buried, and that more for our sakes than its own. Or have it burned, or thrown to the beasts for food; but these reverences, tombs, prayers, praises, are not proper to it at all; they are only the tributes stupidity pays to pride, and are made to be destroyed by philosophy. Here is something that quite contradicts ancient and modern religions; but you are not the ones to whom it must be proved that there is no absurdity like religions, founded as they are on the obnoxious falsehood of the immortality of the soul and on the ridiculous existence of God. No stupidity but that they have reverenced it; and you, my friends, you know better than I that in examining a human institution, the first thing to do is to put any religious idea on one side, as the poison of philosophy.'

'I am in perfect agreement with our friend,' said Clairwil, 'but the strange thing is that there have been libertines who have been passionately addicted to this scheme. I frequently saw in Paris a man who paid their weight in gold for the bodies of boys and girls who had met with violent death and had just been laid in the earth. He had these fresh corpses fetched to his house and committed endless horrors on them.'

'*Il y a longtemps, dis-je, que l'on sait que la jouissance d'un individu récemment assassiné est véritablement très voluptuese le resserrement de l'anus y est, pour les hommes, infiniment plus entier.*'

'What is more,' said Clairwil, 'there is in that sort of imaginary desecration that is most exciting, and I should certainly try it if my sex were not against me.'

'This eccentricity must lead to murder,' I said to my friends.

143

'The man who finds worthwhile pleasure in a corpse is very close to the act that increases them.'

'That may be,' said Clairwil, 'but what matter! If killing's a great pleasure, you will agree that it is but a very small ill.'

And, as the sun was sinking, we hurried to return to Pozzuoli, through the ruins of Cicero's magnificent house.

7

A carriage and six brought us to the foot of the volcano. There we found guides whose practice is to attach you to supporting braces, and by these you ascend the mountain; it takes two hours to reach the summit. The new shoes you bring for this climb are scorched at the end of it. We climbed in good heart, bantering with Olympe, and the unfortunate creature must have completely misunderstood the double meaning, as treacherous as it was involved, of the sarcasms we let fly at her.

This mountain journey was a dreadful task. We were in ashes to the neck all the time; and for every four paces gained, we fell back half-a-dozen, and with the perpetual fear that some lava stream would engulf us alive. We arrived worn out, and we rested as soon as we were at the mouth. It was here that we contemplated, with considerable interest, the placid opening of this volcano that could make the kingdom of Naples tremble in its moments of fury.

'Do you think,' we asked our guides, 'that there is anything to fear today?'

'No,' they replied, 'a few pieces of bitumen, sulphur, or pumice stone might perhaps come up, but in all likelihood there will be no eruption.'

'Well,' said Clairwill 'give us the basket with our refreshment in it, and go down to the village. We are spending the day here, we want to sketch and survey the district.'

'But what if something happens?'

'Didn't you say that nothing is happening?'

'We cannot be sure of that.'

'Well, if anything does happen, we can see the village where you joined us, and we will be down there in no time . . . '

And four or five coins that we slipped into their hands soon decided them to leave us.

They were barely four hundred paces away when I [Juliette] whispered to my friend,

'Shall we use cunning?'

'No,' she replied, 'force.'

And the two of us hurled ourselves on Olympe:

'Whore!' we cried, 'we are tired of you. We only brought you here to get rid of you. . . . We are going to throw you into the heart of the volcano alive.'

'Oh, what have I done?'

'Nothing. You bore us, isn't that enough?'

And as we said that we gagged her with a handkerchief and promptly stifled her cries and jeremiads. Then Clairwil tied her hands with silk cord she had brought for this purpose, and I did the same to her feet. When she was defenseless, we diverted ourselves by watching her; tears escaped from her splendid eyes and came falling on her lovely breast. We undressed her, handled and tormented her everywhere; *nous molestâmes sa belle gorge, nous fustigeâmes son charmant cul, nous lui piquâmes les fesses, nous épilâmes sa motte; je lui mordis le clitoris jusqu'au sang.*

At last, after two hours of the most fearful inflictions, we raised her by the cords and threw her into the middle of the volcano, from out of which we could hear the sound – for more than six minutes – of her body hurtling and plunging by starts and bounds over the sharp angles that tossed it from one to the other, tearing her to shreds. Gradually the noise subsided . . . in the end we could hear nothing more.

'It's over,' said Clairwil, *qui n'avait cessé de se branler depuis qu'elle avait lâché le corps.* 'Oh! foutre, *mon amour, déchargeons maintenant toutes deux, étendues sur le bourpelet même du volcan.* We have just committed a crime here, one of those delightful acts that men think to call atrocious; well, if this act really outrages Nature, let her revenge herself if she can; let an eruption occur at once under our feet, a lava stream open and swallow us. . . . '

I was in no state to reply, already being in a state of intoxication; *je rendais au centuple, a mon amie, les pollutions dont elle m'accoblait. Nous ne parlions plus. Etroitement serrées dans les bras l'une de lautre, nous branlant comme deux tribades.* It was as if we would exchange souls by means of our hot sighs. A few lewd words, a few blasphemies were the only utterances to escape us. We reviled, dared, and defied Nature; and in all the triumph of impunity her weakness and indifference left us, we seemed only to use her indulgence to provoke her more sorely.

'So you see, Juliette,' Clairwil said to me, as she was the first to recover from our frenzy, 'if Nature is provoked by the so-called crimes of man, she could swallow us, and we would both die wrapped in pleasure. . . . But has she done so? Oh rest assured, no crime in the world is capable of drawing the wrath of Nature upon us; all crimes serve her purpose, all are useful to her; and when she inspires us, do not doubt but that she has need of them.'

Clairwil had scarcely finished when a cloud of stones shot from the volcano and rained upon us.

'Aha!' I exclaimed, without troubling to rise, 'Olympe's revenge! These scraps of sulphur and bitumen are her farewells, to tell us that she is already in the bowels of the earth.'

'Quite a simple phenomenon,' replied Clairwil. 'Whenever a solid body falls to the heart of the volcano, it sets up a slight eruption by stirring the matter that perpetually seethes deep in its womb.'

'Let nothing disturb us, let us dine, Clairwil, and consider yourself mistaken over the cause of that rain of stones that has just showered on us. It is no other than Olympe asking for her clothes. We must give them back.'

And after taking the gold and the jewels, we made a packet of the lot, and threw it into the same hole that had just admitted our unfortunate friend. Then we dined. There was silence, the crime was achieved, and Nature content. We went down, and found our attendants at the foot of the mountain.

PENSEE

To man, God is precisely what colors are to a man borne blind, impossible for him to imagine. The reply you get to that is that those colors exist all the same, and that if the blind man does not imagine them it is due to his lack of a sense, not due to the thing's nonexistence; and similarly, that if man does not comprehend God it is due to his lack of some sense, not due to that being's uncertainty of existence.

Now here is the crux of the sophism, for the names, the properties of, and the differences between, colors are merely matters of convention that derive from the necessity our senses place us in to differentiate among them, while the question of their existence is frivolous, that is to say, it is highly frivolous of us to dispute whether a ribbon dyed brown is really brown: nothing is real in all that but our conventions. And so with God, who is presented to our imaginations precisely as color is to the brains of blind men, that is, as something one is told about but which nothing proves the reality of, and consequently may very well not be at all – just as, when you present a ribbon to a blind person assuring

146

him it is brown, you not only give him no idea of it but you tell him, moreover, nothing he cannot deny, regardless of all you might argue or be capable of arguing to convince him. Similarly, when you speak to man about God, not only do you give him no idea of it but you bring to his imagination, moreover, only something he is capable of denying, combatting or destroying, while you are left without the smallest real argument with which to persuade him.

God, then, no more exists for man than colors do for men born blind, and man is, then as right to maintain there is no God as the blind man is to hold that there are no colors, for colors are not real things but simply matters of convention and all matters of convention acquire reality in men's minds only in so far as they affect their senses and are capable of being understood by them. Thus, a thing may very well be real in the eyes of all men equipped with their five senses and yet become doubtful or even nonexistent to him who lacks the sense necessary for its conception, while the thing that is utterly incomprehensible, utterly impossible for the senses to perceive, becomes nonexistent – as nonexistent as color becomes to the blind man. Consequently, if color is nonexistent to the blind man because he lacks the necessary sense for assuming it, then God is nonexistent to man because none of his senses is capable of perceiving it and this God has, then, not even a conventional existence like color but in itself no reality whatever. A society of blind men, lacking the guidance of other men, would similarly have conventional names to express things without reality; with reference to this fine chimera that we qualify with the name of God, we are that society of blind men: we have imagined a thing we believed necessary but which has no existence other than our own need to create it.

Measured by this same yardstick, all principles of human morality would similarly be reduced to nothing, for all duties, being simply conventions, are similarly chimerical. Man said such and such a thing will be virtue because it is useful to me, such and such another will be vice because it harms me: these are the futile conventions of blind men's society whose laws have no intrinsic reality. The true way to judge our weakness relative to Nature's sublime mysteries is to judge by the weakness of beings who have one sense fewer than we. Their errors with respect to us are our errors with respect to Nature: the blind man sets up his conventions according to his needs and the mediocrity of his faculties, while ordinary men have similarly made their laws in accordance with their little knowledge, their little views, and their little needs. But there is nothing real in all that, nothing that could not be either misunderstood by a society inferior to ours in faculties, or formally denied by one that surpassed our own by its possession of more delicate organs or additional senses.

How hateful our laws, our virtues, our vices, our divinities would be in the eyes of a society possessing two or three more senses than we and a sensitivity double our own – for such a society would be more perfect and closer to Nature. Consequently the most perfect being we could conceive would be the one who would depart most radically from our conventions and would consider them most hateful – as we consider those of a society inferior to us. When we follow this chain of reasoning and arrive at Nature herself, we shall easily understand that everything we say, everything we order and assume, is as far from the perfection of her views and as inferior to her as are the laws of a society of blind men in relation to our own.

Without the senses, no ideas, *nihil est (in) intellectu, quod non prius fuerit in sensu* is, in a word, the great foundation and the great truth the preceding argument establishes, and it is fantastic that M. Nicole attempted in his logic to destroy this proven axiom of all philosophy. There come into our minds, he claims, other ideas than those acquired through the senses, and one of these great ideas which can occur to us, apart from the senses, is *I think, therefore I am.*

This idea, the author says, has no color, no odor and thus is not the product of the senses – is it possible so to bury oneself in the dust of the school as to reason with this degree of falseness? Certainly this idea, *I think, therefore I am,* is not of the species 'this table is whole' – because the sense of touch proves it to my mind. It is not, I grant, due to the operation of any one particular sense but is the result of them all – and really so, for if a creature without senses could exist, it would be totally impossible for it to formulate this thought, *I think, therefore I am.* Consequently this thought is the result of the operation of all our senses, although not of any one in particular, and therefore it cannot destroy the great, infallible reasoning as to the impossibility of our acquiring ideas apart from our senses. Religion, I grant you, does not agree, but religion is the thing in the world one should consult least on the subject of philosophy, because it is religion that most obscures all priciples and most shamefully bows man down under the ridiculous yoke of faith, destroyer of all truths.

148

Petrarch is all my consolation here. I read him with a pleasure,
an avidity to which nothing can be compared. But with it I do
what Madame de Sévigné did with her daughter's letters, *I read
slowly for fear of having done*. How well constructed this work is!...
Laura turns my head; I am like a child with her; all day I read and
at night I dream of her. Listen to a dream I had of her yesterday
while the whole world was at its pleasures.

It was about midnight. I had just fallen asleep, her memoirs in
my hand. Suddenly she appeared to me ... I saw her! The horrors
of the tomb had not altered the splendor of her charms, and her
eyes had as much fire as when Petrarch praised them. Black crape
covered her entirely, and her beautiful blond hair floated negligen-
tly above. It seemed that love, in order to make her more beautiful,
had wished to soften the lugubrious apparel in which she met my
eyes. 'Why do you lie groaning on the floor?' she said to me. 'Come
and rejoin me. No more evils, no more sorrows, no more care in
the limitless space where I dwell. Take courage and follow me
there.' At these words I threw myself at her feet; I said to her. 'Oh
my Mother!' ... and sobs choked my voice. She held out a hand to
me that I covered with tears; she wept too. 'When I lived in this
world that you detest,' she added, 'I amused myself looking into
the future; I imagined my descendents down to you, *but I did
not see you so wretched*.' Then, full of my despair and affection,
I threw my arms about her neck to stay her, or to follow her, and
to water her with my tears, but the phantom vanished. There
remained only my sorrow.

> *O voi che travagliate, ecco il cammino*
> *Venite a me se'l passo altri non serra.*
> Petr: son. LIX

Goodnight, my dear one, I love you and embrace you with all
my heart. Have then a little more pity for me, I beg you, for I
swear to you that I am more wretched than you think. Consider
all this that I suffer, and the state of my soul has all the melancholy of my imagination. I embrace even those who frown on me,
because in them I hate only their faults.

This 17 February, at the end of two years of frightful chains.

PART III

Chronology and Bibliography

A BRIEF CHRONOLOGY
OF SADE'S LIFE

1740   *June* 2 – The Countess de Sade, neé (1712) Marie-Eléonore de Maillé de Carman, lady-in-waiting to the Princess de Condé, gives birth to a son[1] in the Condés residence, Rue de Condé, Paris. This is in the seventh year of her marriage to Jean-Baptiste-Joseph-François, Count de Sade,[2] born in 1702, Governor-General of the provinces of Bresse, Burgey, Valromey, and Gex, seigneur of Samane and La Coste coseigneur of Mazun.

      June 3   In the absence of his godparents, the child is baptized by proxy in the parish church of Saint-Sulpice, Paris, receiving the Christian names Donatien-Alphonse. François.[3]

1745   *January* 24 – Jacques-François-Paul-Aldonse de Sade,[4] the Marquis' uncle, takes up residence at the Benedictine monastery of Saint-Léger d'Ebreuil as Abbé. He is entrusted with the education of his nephew.

1750   The Marquis returns to Paris to enter the Jesuit College d'Harcourt. His private tutor is the Abbé Amblet.

1754   *May* 24 – The Marquis de Sade obtains letters patent of nobility from a genealogist to secure admission to the Light Cavalry of the King's Guard.

1755   *December* 5 – He is promoted to Sub-Lieutenant unpaid in the Royal Regiment of Foot.

1757   *January* 14 – He is commissioned as *Lieutenant des Carabiniers, color-*bearer.[5]

1758   *April* 21 – He is promoted to Captain in the Calvalry Regiment de Bourgogne.

1763   *March* 15 – The Marquis is retired from the Army.
      May 1 – Royal assent is given to the proposed marriage

between the Marqis de Sade, allied by the Maillé family to the royal-blooded Condés, and Renée-Pélagie Cordier de Launay de Montreuil, born in 1741, and daughter of M. de Montreuil, President of the Board of Excise at Paris.
May 17 – The marriage takes place in the church of Saint-Roch, two days after signature of the contract.
October 29 – The Marquis de Sade, by command of the King, is committed to prison[6] in the château de Vincennes for excesses in a *petite maison* he has been frequenting since June.
November 13 – He is set free, but ordered to retire to his father-in-law's château in Normandy.

1764   *May*   4 – The Marquis succeeds his father in the *Parlement de Bourgogne* in his office of Governor-General.
September 8 – Sade is in Paris, in debt to the extent of 4,500 francs, and living for the greater part of the time with a dancer from the Opéra. Her name is Beauvoisin. The Marquise is unaware of these escapades.
November 30 – Marais, Inspector of Police, issues a report in which he notes that, M. de Sade being in Paris, 'I strongly advised the woman Brissaut, without going into details not to supply him with girls to go with him in *petites maisons*'
1765(?)*November* – He takes the dancer Beauvoisin to La Coste, and passes her off as his wife.

1767   *January* 24 – Death of the Comte de Sade. The Marquis is sole heir to his father's estate and offices.
April 20 – Sade leaves for Lyons to rejoin Mlle. Beauvoisin, while his wife, five months pregnant, is in Paris.
August   27 – Louis-Marie, Comte de Sade,[7] the Marquis' first-born, is born in Paris.
October 16 – Report by Marais: 'It will not be long before talk of further outrages by M. le comte [*sic*] de Sade reaches our ears. He is doing his utmost to induce Mlle. Rivière, from the Opéra, to live with him; and he has offered her 25 francs a month, on condition that she spend such days as she is not on the stage at his *petite maison* at Arcueil. The young lady has refused.'

1768   *April* 3 – The following deposition was made against the Marquis de Sade relating to the events of this day:
'Rose Kailair,[8] widow of Charles Valentin, pastry-cook's man, she being a cotton spinner, aged thirty-six or there-

154

abouts, residing in Paris, Rue Soly, parish St. Eustache, witness summoned by writ of yesterday's date by Griveau, court-bailiff, a copy of which she has showed us.

After taking oath to tell the truth:

Reading to her of the said declaration, indictment, and adjudication of the Court:

Stated not be related, connected, servant or domestic of the parties, save that the Sr. de Sade had wanted to engage her in his service, and taken her for this purpose into his house at Arcueil, nevertheless without her being agreed as to any wages.

Deposes that on last Easter Sunday, having heard Mass in the Petits Pères on the Place des Victoires, leaving Mass and going out to the Place des Victoires, an individual having given her alms, another individual who was near the railings of the said Place, dressed in a gray frock coat, a hunting-knife at his side, grasping a cane, and a whitish muff, called her, and proposed she should earn a crown if she would come with him; that having replied to him that she was not what he thought, he told her that it was to do his room, and that she had only to follow him; that in effect she followed him until near the new part of la Halle, and he made her enter a room on the second floor (so she believes) which room was furnished in yellow damask with a chaise longue which she believes was of the same material, but covered like the armchairs with a cloth cover. That having made her sit down he asked her if she would like to come into the country, to which she replied that she did not care where she earned her living. Then he left her, telling her that he still had several visits to make and that he would come and fetch her in an hour; that in fact one hour later he returned with a cab which he made her get into and closed the windows which were of wood. That while they were there, he said nothing to her but if she knew where he was taking her, to which she replied that she could not know because she could see nothing. That he had the cab stop near the village of Arcueil. That in getting out he instructed the coachman to take care of something he had put in his carriage, and told the witness to follow him; that this individual passed by the main entrance, led the witness to a small green door farther away, and told her to wait at this door; that afterwards he entered by the main door, and came to open the small one to her; that beyond this he made her go through a small garden, and took her into

155

a high room that looked over the large garden, and in which there were two beds and some straw-bottomed chairs; that he told her to stay there and that he was going to find a piece of bread for her and something to drink and she was not to grow weary, and he went away after having shut her in with double locks; that about an hour later he came to open the door, and he said to her come down, my dear; which she did; and he led her across the same small garden she came in by, into a closet the door of which he shut, and told her to undress; that she asked him why, he replied that it was for enjoyment; that having reminded him that it was not for that he had made her come, he said that if she did not undress, he would kill her and bury her himself; that after he had gone out and left her alone, she undressed, and was not entirely so when he returned; and having found her still in her shift, he said it must also come off, to which having replied that she would rather die, he himself tore off the said shift making it pass over the head of the witness; after which he led her into another room next to that one, and in the middle of which there was a divan of red chintz with a white spot, threw her on the said bed on her front, tied her by the four limbs with hempen cord, put a bolster on her neck, witness observing that when he came to fetch her from the closet to take her into the said room he had taken off his coat and his shirt, and had put on a sleeveless vest, and tied a white handkerchief around his head, and that when she entered the said room the curtains were drawn. That being attached to the bed he took a birch with which he whipped her, made various incisions with a small knife or penknife, poured red wax and white wax in a greater quantity on these wounds, after which he began to beat her again, to make incisions and pour wax, all of which ill-treatment he repeated up to seven or eight times. That the witness having shouted from the time of these ill-treatments he showed her a knife, and menaced her, if she cried, with killing her and burying her himself as she has already told us; that she then ceased to cry out. Witness adds that on each occasion when he birched her, he also gave her blows with a stick. That in the middle of her torture the witness made various protests to him, and had begged him not to let her die because she had not taken Easter Sacrament, to which he replied that he would confess her himself; that having told him that she could not confess herself to him

156

and having made still further protests to him, he set about uttering very loud and frightening cries and cut the cords that bound her, and took her back to the closet to dress again; he brought her a jug of water with a large salad bowl to wash in, and that at this moment she had already recovered her shift and her skirt, that she washed herself, and wiped herself with a towel that he had brought as well, and that this towel being found all bloody, he had made her wash it. That he then brought her a small phial in which there was a liquid the color of *eau de vie*, and told her to rub herself with it, and that in an hour it would disappear; that she rubbed herself with it in all the cicatrized parts, and that this caused her very sharp pains. That being completely dressed again, he brought her a small piece of bread, a piece of cold stock-beef, about half a liter of wine in a bottle, and then took her back to the room upstairs, the witness taking the bread, the plateful, the bottle, and a goblet. That he shut her in the said room after telling her not to go near the casement window, not to show herself, and not to make any noise, and that he would let her leave towards evening; upon which she asked him to release her early because she did not know where she was, and that she had no money, and that she did not want to sleep in the street; to which he replied that she had no call to be worried. After which he went away and shut her in the said room of which the witness secured the door by a hook that was inside; then she took two bedcovers which were on the two beds of the said room, and having unpicked with her knife one side of the shutter of the casement window which overlooks the garden, she attached by large pins the two bedcovers to an oak crossbar that in the center of the said window and slid them into the garden, from where she reached a wall, which she scaled with the help of trellises that were by a garden bower, fell into a large close and hurt her arm and left hand in falling, and from the close reached the street; that a servant ran after her telling her to come back and that his master wanted to reach an agreement with her, which she refused to do; upon which the said servant drew out a purse and said he was going to give her money which she refused in like manner. Witness points out to us that she was able to tell that he had poured red wax on her in that having found a way of loosening the bonds with her left hand, and having moved it to her back, red wax fell on it, and that also in washing she found a considerable amount of wax in the basin. That she encountered some women from the village who assisted her and took her to the château, where she stayed until five days after the arrangement she made; which is all she claims to know, her deposition having been read, witness when summoned stated that it contained the truth, adhered to it, claimed taxing, and declared herself unable to write or sign the summons following the warrant. Approved, six words deleted.

Chavane   Lebreton.'

In giving evidence, the Marquis de Sade denied the crueler points of Rose Keller's evidence, but admitted the main events.

April 7 – Rose Keller is persuaded to withdraw her charge on an idemnity of 2,400 francs and seven *louis d'or* for dressings and medicaments.

April 12 – The Marquis is in detention at the château de Saumur.

April 30 – Inspector Marais transfers the Marquis to the Fortress of Pierre-Encise, near Lyons.

June 2 – He is transferred to the Concieggeri prison in Paris.

June 10 – The accused is examined and admits the principal events and the motive of *libertinage*. On the same day, Parliament ratifies letters of annulment the Marquis has obtained from the King. He is fined 100 francs.

1769   *June* 27 – Birth of Donatien-Claude-Armand, Chevalier de Sade, second son of the Marquis.

1771   *March* 13 – The Marquis obtains a commission as Colonel of Cavalry.

April 17 – Birth of Madeleine-Laure, daughter of the Marquis.

September 9 – Sade leaves Fort-l'Evêque, a debtor's prison, where he has been for a week.

1772   *June* 25 – The Marquis is in Marseille to collect funds, and orders Latour, his lackey, to recruit prostitutes for his two days' stay.

June 27 – At ten o'clock in the morning, de Sade, 'handsome, full-faced . . . wearing a blue-lined gray dress coat, a jacket, and marigold-colored breeches . . . with sword,

158

hunting-knife, and cane' entered with his lackey the room of a prostitute named Borelly, and known as Mariette, on the third floor of an apartment-building.[9] There are three others present: Rose Coste (aged 18), Marianette Laugier (aged 20), and Marianne Laverne (aged 18); Mariette is 23. Mutual flagellation takes place; *paedicacio* is proposed to the women and refused, according to them, and other sexual enjoyments not specified in later statements. Cantharidized aniseed is offered by Sade and taken. The same evening at nine o'clock Sade visits Marguerite Coste, (aged 19) in the Rue Saint-Ferréol-le-Vieux; *paedicacio* aniseed.

June 30 – Marguerite Coste, who has had liberal helpings of the the Marquis' confectionery, has been 'suffering internal pains for several days,' and believes herself poisoned by the aniseed. She makes a statement before the magistrate; a surgeon is appointed to examine her, and an apothecary named to analyze her feces.[10]

July 1 – The first four prostitutes make depositions complaining of alimentary pains and unworthy conduct in their clients, whom they accuse of heterosexual sodomy.

July 4 – The public prosecutor issues warrants for the arrest of Sade and Latour.

July 11 – The Château of La Coste is searched, the seigneur's goods and chattels seized, and an inventory made. The accused are found to have fled several days before.

September 3 – The public prosecutor's sentence at Marseille: Sade and Latour are condemned to make due apology in front of the cathedral door before being taken to the Place Saint-Louis where 'the said Sr. de Sade is to be beheaded on a scaffold and the said Latour hung and strangled on a gibbet . . . then the body of the the said Sr de Sade and that of the said Latour shall be burnt and their ashes thrown to the wind. . . .' The crime is stated to be 'poisoning and sodomy.'

September 12 – Sade and Latour are executed and burnt in effigy at Aix.

October 27 – The Marquis arrives at Chambéry.

December 5 – At the instance of his mother-in-law, Madame de Montreuil, Sade and his servant are arrested by command of the King of Sardinia, Duke of Savoy.

December 9 – He is sent to the Fortress of Miolans, and signs a promise not to attempt to escape.

1773   *March* 5 – Madame de Sade arrives at Chambéry, and being refused accesss to Miolans, attempts to enter disguised as a man, but without success.
April 30 – The Marquis, his servant, and a fellow prisoner escape in the night.
May 1 – Sade arrives at Grenoble.

1774   *January* 6 – An officer, constables, and mounted constabulary enter La Coste during the night, but find only the Marquise. The chateau is searched and the officer burns or confiscates papers found in the Marquis' room.
November – The Marquis has been living at La Coste in the utmost seclusion.

1775   *May* 3 – Complaints of rape and seduction are made against the Marquis by young persons from Vienne and Lyon.
May 11 – Anne Sablonnière, known as Nanon, a chambermaid at the château, gives birth to a daughter she atributes to the Marquis. The child lives three months.
June 20 – The Prior of the Monastery of Jumiège informs the Abbé de Sade that he has given asylum to a girl escaped from La Coste, and that three servants have come from there to take her away, on the pretext that she has stolen 40 francs. She and others from the château are placed under the Abbé's protection. The Abbé has recently insisted that his nephew be shut up as mad.
June 22 – The Prior confirms to the Abbé that he has suppressed injurious rumors, but that the Marquis must be confined for the rest of his days. He is convinced that the Marquise is no better than her husband, as he is aware that none of the household takes Easter Sacrament, and that she allows her young servants to have intercourse with a married woman who is a Lutheran.
August 10 – The Marquis writes from Italy, where he is traveling incognito, under the name Comte de Mazan.
September 29 – He arives at Rome.

1776   *January* – Sade is in Naples, where the French *chargé d'affairs* takes him for a fugitive cashier. He is obliged to reveal his identity, and is presented at Court in the uniform of a French Colonel.
May 4 – *end of June* – He travels to Rome, Bologna, Turin, and Grenoble.

November 2 – The Marquis is at Montepellier, where Father Durand, entrusted with finding a female cook for La Coste, vouches for the respectability of the château to Trillet (or Treillet), a blanket-weaver, who agrees to his twenty-two-year-old daughter Catherine being engaged in this capacity.

November 4 – The Marquis returns to La Coste.

Mid-December – Sade appears to have written to Father Durand to ask him to bring a chambermaid, an undercook, a barber, and a secretary to La Coste. They arrive with the Father, but only the undercook remains, and the rest return to Montpellier the following morning.

1777 *January* 14 – Death of the dowager Countess de Sade, the Marquis' mother.

January 17 – About one o'clock in the afternoon, Trillet arrives to reclaim his daughter Catherine, known as Justine in the château. During a dispute, Trillet fires a pistol almost at point-blank range at the Marquis. The shot misses, and Trillet flees. About five o'clock the same afternoon, Catherine attempts to pacify her father, who has been brought back to the château, and who, his fury unabated, again fires his pistol in the courtyard.

Late January – On investigation of the attempted murder, Trillet produces evidence, from the servants who fled, that the Marquis 'tried to lay hands on their persons, offering them a purse of money.' In the meantime, Father Durand has been dismissed from his monastery. Sade categorically denies Trillet's statements.

February 13 – The Marquis is arrested and taken by Marais to Vincennes, where he is incarcerated.

1778 *May* 27 – The King annuls the Marquis de Sade's arrest *in absentia* in September, 1772.

July 14 – After public cross-examination, Sade is bound over to behave more decently, and is forbidden by decree of the Parliament of Provence to live in or frequent Marseille for a period of three years.

July 18 – He is at La Coste.

August 19 – Warned of suspicious strangers in the locality, Sade takes to a vagrant life in the district.

August 26 – Returning to the château, the Marquis is arrested at dawn by Marais with a heavy escort, who are witnessed committing outrages against their prisoner.

September 7 – He arrives at Vincennes in the evening.

December – After three months' confinement, the prisoner is permitted to receive pens and paper and to take the air twice a week.

1779   *January* – The Marquis sends New Year verses to Mlle. de Rousset.[11]

1780   *April* 25 – The prisoner is now allowed daily exercise.

1781   *July* 13 – The Marquis is visited by his wife for the first time.

1782   *July* 12 – He finishes the notebook containing his *Dialogue entre un prêtre et un moribond*.

September 25 – Madame de Sade's visits cease on account of the prisoner's conduct. Her visits had previously been stopped in October, 1781, on account of her husband's raging jealousy.

1783   *February* – Sade is treated by an oculist.

1784   *February* 29 – He is transferred to the Bastille.

1785   *November* 28 – He finishes *Les 120 Journées de Sodome* after 37 days' work, writing it out on a long roll of paper measuring about 13 yards by $4\frac{1}{2}$ inches, using both sides.

1786   *July* 13 – His wife's visits are re-established, one a month.

1787   *July* 8 – In spite of eye trouble, *Les Infortunes de la Vertu* is concluded after 15 days' writing.

1788   *March* 1 – *Eugénie de Franval* is begun and finished in 8 days.

November 24 – Over and above his evening exercise for one hour, the prisoner is permitted a daily morning walk of the same duration. He is allowed to receive his wife either for one hour every week, or for two hours every two weeks.

1789   *July* 2 – From the *Répertoire ou journalier du château de la Bastille*: 'The Count de Sade shouted through his window, on several occasions, that the prisoners of the Bastille were having their throats cut, and that he should be released.'

July 4 – Sade is transferred to Charenton, and seals are affixed to his room in the Bastille.

July 14 – Madame de Sade, unable to be present as asignee for the unsealing of the Marquis' room, leaves for the country. In the meantime his room is ransacked.

1790   *April* 2 – Sade gains his liberty and leaves Charenton. He is absolutely without resources.

April 3 – Madam de Sade, at the Convent of Sainte-Aure, refuses to see her husband, from whom she wishes to part.

August 17 – Sade reads his play *Le Mari Crédule* at the Comédie-Française.

August 25 – He forms a liaison with a young actress, Marie-Constance Renelle, a wife who has been forsaken with her child.

September 23 – Sade states his agreement, before a lawyer to a decree of separation from his wife by default.

1791   *June* 12 – His novel, *Justine ou les Malheurs de la Vertu*, is with the printers, and published this year.

October 22 – First performance, at the Théâtre Molière, of *Le Comte Oxtiern ou les Effets du Libertinage*.

1792   *September* 3 – He is secretary of his *Section des Piques* during the massacres.

September 17 - 21 – Natives of La Coste and Apt break into the château to loot and ravage it, the *garde nationale* being powerless to oppose them. Some furniture and goods are rescued from destruction by the municipal authorities and removed, only to be later requisitioned by two citizens of Apt.

October 17 – Sade is a soldier of the 8th Company of the *Section des Piques* and is charged with organizing its cavalry.

1793   *December* 5 – Sade, suspected of moderantism, is arrested by the police of the Commune, and is taken to Madelonnettes.

1794   *January* 13 – He is transferred to Carmes.

Janury 22 – He is transferred to Saint-Lazare.

March 23 – 'François-Aldonze-Donacien-Louis Sade, aged

54 years, 5 feet 2 inches in height, medium nose, small mouth, round chin, light gray hair, oval face, bare high forehead, pale blue eyes.'

March 27 – Ill, he is transferred to Picpus Hospital.
October 15 – He is set free.

1795   In this year, *La Philosophie dans le Boudoir* is published. *August* 26 – The eight volumes of *Aline et Valcour* are published.

1796   *October* 13 – Sade signs the bill of sale to Rovère, the 'People's Member,' of his château and lands at La Coste, for the sum of 58,400 livres, which was never to be paid him in full.

1797   *June* 18 – Sade is traveling in Provence on business, with Madame Quesnet, to whose house in Paris he moved the previous December.

1798   *September* 10 – Now completely penniless, Sade and Madame Quesnet part company, and he takes refuge with one of his farmers in Beauce.

1799   *February* 13 – He is earning 40 sous a day working at the entertainments at Versailles. He lives in a garret with Madame Quesnet's son, Charles.
December 13 – *Oxtiern* is revived at Versailles, and Sade plays the part of Farbrice.

1800   *January* 26 – 'Dying of cold and hunger,' he is in hospital at Versailles.
July – *Publication* of *Zoloé*, and anonymous pamphlet aimed at Joséphine, Bonaparte, and others.

1801   *March* 6 – Arrest of Sade and his publisher, Massé, with whom he was found during the house-search that brought to light several copies of *Justine* and *Juliette* annotated in his own hand, and several autograph manuscripts, including. *Justine*. At the same time, another search is made in Madame Quesnet's house in Saint-Ouen, where Sade has a secret closet 'furnished with wall hangings depicting the most obscene subjects, for the most part drawn from the infamous novel *Justine*,' and which are removed to the Préfecture.

April 5 – Sade incarcerated at Sainte-Pélagie.

1802 *May* 20 – He writes to the Minister of Justice that after fifteen months' detention in the most frightful prison in Paris, he wishes to be set free or sentenced. He swears he is not the author of *Justine*.

1803 *April* 27 – He is transferred to the asylum at Charenton.

1804 *September* 8 – A report made to the Minister of Police considers Sade 'an incorrigible man' in a perpetual state of 'sexual dementia,' and whose 'character is inimical to all obedience.' Its finding is that 'there are grounds for leaving him at Charenton, where his family pays his lodging, and where, for the sake of their honor, they wish him to stay.'

1806 *January* 30 – Sade makes his will. The last[12] clause runs: '5. Finally, I utterly forbid the opening of my body on any pretext whatsoever. I most earnestly entreat that it be kept in the room in which I shall die for forty-eight hours, and placed in a wooden bier that shall only be nailed up at the end of the forty-eight hours prescribed above, on the expiration of which the said bier shall be nailed up; during this interval, an express letter shall be sent to M. Le Normand, timber merchant, No. 101, Boulevard de l'Egalité, in Versailles, to request him to call in person with a cart to take my body under his escort to the wood on my lands at Malmaison, in the parish of Mancé, near Epernon, where I wish it to be laid, without ceremony of any kind, in the first thick coppice to be found to the right in the said wood on entering it from the side of the former château by the main avenue that divides it. The grave dug in this coppice shall be opened by the farm-tenant of Malmaison, under the surveillance of M. Le Normand, who shall not leave my body until he has laid it in the said grave; if he so desires, he may be joined in this ceremony by those of my relatives or friends who, with no kind of funeral trappings whatsoever, have wished to accord me this last token of affection. Once the grave is covered, it shall be sown over with acorns, so that the plot of the said grave being restored in the course of time, and the coppice being thick again as heretofore, all trace of my tomb shall disappear from the

165

upper surface of the earth, as I pride myself that my memory shall be effaced from the minds of men, with the exception nontheless of the small number of those who have loved me to the last and whose tender memory I bear to the grave.

Made this thirtieth day of January eighteen hundred and six at Charenton-Saint-Maurice, being sound in mind and body.

[signed] D.A.F. Sade.'

1807   *April* 25 – Sade finished his fair copy of the *Histore d'Emilie*, which fills 72 notebooks and constitutes the last 4 volumes of a vast work in 10 volumes which has the general title of *Les Journées de Florabelle ou la Nature dévoilée, suivies des Mémoires de l'abbé de Modose et des Aventures d'Emilie de Volnange.*
June 5 – The police search his rooms at Charenton.

1808   *August* 2 – Royer-Collard, head surgeon of the asylum at Charenton, points out to the Minister of Police the inconvenience of Sade's presence: 'This man is by no means mad. Vice is his only frenzy . . . the general rumor here is that he is cohabiting with a woman [Madame Quesnet] who passes as his daughter.' He recommends the suppression of Sade's theatrical organization as harmful to the patients, and requests his transfer to some other place of confinement.
September 11 – Following this report, the police decide to transfer him to Ham, but this decision is reversed the next day.

1809   *June* 9 – Louis-Marie de Sade, the elder son of the Marquis, is killed in ambush in Italy.

1810   *July* 7 – Death of the Marquise de Sade.

October 18 – The Home Secretary issues two departmental orders: (1) seeing that Sade 'is suffering from the most dangerous of all mental disorders' and that his writings 'are no less bereft of reason than his speech and actions,' the Minister decrees that he be placed in complete isolation, so that all communication with him is prohibited and that 'the greatest care is taken to forbid him the use of pencils, ink, pens, and paper,' the director of the asylum being personally responsible for carrying out this decision; (2) 'Seeing that Charenton asylum is only designed for the treatment and confinement of lunatics' and 'that if *le suier de Sade*, not being in a state of complete lunacy, may nevertheless be considered as suffering from a special kind of madness which does not permit his continued freedom in society,' the Minister decrees identical measures, but with no mention of the forbidding of his writing.

October 24 – The director of Charenton acknowledges his instructions and replies that he has no place of isolation and would be 'humiliated to be a jailer.'

1811   *February* 6 – The police report unfavourably on bookshops that are steadily selling, in Paris and the provinces, *La Nouvelle Justine*, and engravings detached from this work.

1812   *June* 9 – Following sessions of the Privy Council, His Majesty confirms Sade's detention.

       October 6 – Occasional couplets, written by Sade, are sung before the Archbishop of Paris on his visit to Charenton.

1813   *May* 6 – All theatrical shows are forbidden at Charenton, by ministerial order.

1814   *December* 1 – Sade can no longer walk. His health has been failing for some time.

       December 2 – Armand de Sade arrives to see his sick father and begs M. Ramon, the house physician, to attend him. Sade's breathing is labored and stertorous, and becomes more and more congested; towards ten in the evening, shortly after drinking, the Marquis dies peacefully, of a 'pulmonary obstruction' according to Dr. Ramon, or of a 'prostrating and gangrenous fever,' acccording to the subsequent administrative report.

       December 4 or 5 – In defiance of his will, the Marquis is buried religiously in the cemetery of Saint-Maurice, at a cost of 65 francs, of which 20 are for the cross laid upon the nameless grave.

1815   *January* 2 – The inventory of Sade's effects of Charenton is completed. It includes furniture and clothing, mostly in a poor state, 40 francs 50 centimes in cash, a large unframed oil painting of the Marquis' father, four miniatures, bundles of documents, a trunk containing twenty-one

167

different manuscript compositions, and his library. This consisted of 72 works in a total of 269 volumes; among conventional books, history, philosophy, or novels, there are such titles as these: *La Princesse de Cleves*, *Don Quixote*, Rousseau's Works, *Mathematical Recreations*, *L'Art de Communiquer ses Idées*, *L'Art de se Tranquiliser*, *The Chinese Spy*, *Essay on Dangerous Diseases*, the 1785 edition of Voltaire in 89 volumes, *The Pornograph*, a Rhyming Dictionary, *The Man in the Iron Mask*, and so on.

circa 1830 – As the cemetery is being redesigned, Sades' body is exhumed in the presence of Dr Ramon, who removes the cranium. Later it was mislaid by a phrenologist.

[1] The Marquis' known genealogy is considerable. The family, in all probability, was founded by Bertrand de Saze (a village near Avignon), who is heard of *circa* 1216. In the fourteenth century, the Marquis could boast Laura, who was the wife of Hugues de Sade, and who was noticed by Petrarch in Avignon in 1327, and immortalized in his sonnets. Other members of the family were distinguished in the professions, the church, and the army particularly. Elzear de Sade, for services to the Emperor Sigismund, was granted permission to bear the imperial eagle on his coat-of-arms. The device was retained in the family; its heraldic description is 'gules with eight-pointed star in or surmounted by spread-eagle beaked, in sable, talonned, diademed in gules.'

[2] At this time Ambassador from Louis XV to the Elector at Cologne; later, Ambassador to Russia, and then to London.

[3] Apparently by mistake; the intended name seems to have been Louis-Aldonse-Donatien. Aldonse is a Provençal name, and was perhaps misheard by the priest, who inscribed Alphonse.

[4] Born in 1705, he entered the Church and was appointed Vicar-General to the Archbishops of Toulouse and Narbonne in 1735. He moved to Paris, but later retired to Vaucluse, abandoning fashionable literary life; in 1764 he published *Mèmoires sur la Vie de François Pétrarque*, and then a translation of the poet's works. He also wrote *Remarques sur les premiers Poètes Français et les Troubadours*. He died on January 3, 1778.

[5] During the period 1756-1763, he took part in the Seven Years' War and saw active service in Germany.

[6] He was to spend nearly twenty-one years of his life in various prisons.

[7] The titles *Comte* and *Marquis* alternated at each succession in the family.

[8] So spelled; invariably modernized as Rose Keller.

[9] Now 15a, Rue d'Aubagne, Marseille.

[10] No trace of arsenic or sublimate was found, according to the subsequent report.

[11] Marie-Dorothée de Rousset was a governess at La Coste, and in this year she kept up a gallant correspondence with the Marquis. She resumed it in 1781, but died of consumption in 1784, aged 40.

[12] The first four clauses have never been published, but they provide generously for Madame Quesnet.

BIBLIOGRAPHY

I

PRINCIPAL WORKS

1. JUSTINE, OU LES MALHEURS DE LA VERTU. *En Hollande* [Paris], *Chez les Libraires Associés*, 1791.
   2 volumes in 1, 8vo. Frontispiece by Chéry.
   Also an illustrated edition, 12mo, of the same date.

2. JUSTINE, OU LES MALHEURS DE LA VERTU. *A Londres* [Paris, Cazin] 1792.
   2 volumes, 16mo. Frontispiece and five engravings.

3. JUSTINE, OU LES MALHEURS DE LA VERTU. *Troisième* [fourth] *édition, corrigée, et augmentée Philadelphie* [Paris], 1794.
   2 volumes, 16mo. Frontispiece and 5 erotic engravings.

4. JUSTINE, OU LES MALHEURS DE LA VERTU. *A Londres* [Paris], 1797.
   4 volumes, decimo-octavo. 6 erotic engravings. Further augmented edition.

5. LA NOUVELLE JUSTINE, OU LES MALHEURS DE LA VERTU. *Ouvrage orné d'un Frontispice et de quarante Sujets gravés avec soin En Hollande* [Paris], 1779.
   4 volumes, 12mo. The first four volumes of the definitive edition in ten volumes, the last six having as title:
   LA NOUVELLE JUSTINE, OU LES MALHEURS DE LA VERTU, SUIVIE DE L'HISTOIRE DE JULIETTE, SA SOEUR. *Ouvrage orné d'un Frontispice et de cent sujets gravés avec soin.*
   6 volumes, 12mo. Contains 100 erotic engravings in all, i.e. in the ten volumes.

6. ALINE ET VALCOUR, OU LE ROMAN PHILOSOPHIQUE. ECRIT A LA BASTILLE UN AN AVANT LA RÉVOLUTION DE FRANCE. *Orné de quatorze gravures. Par le Citoyen S***. A Paris, chez Girouard, Libraire, rue du Bout-du-Monde, No. 47,* 1793. (Also 1795.)
   8 volumes, 16mo. Also issued with 16 plates, 8 parts in 4 volumes.

7. LA PHILOSOPHIE DANS LE BOUDOIR, *ouvrage posthume* [sic] *de l'auteur de Justine. A Londres* [Paris], aux *dépens de la Compagnie, MDCCXCXV* [1795].
   2 volumes, 16mo. Frontispiece and 4 erotic engravings.

8. OXTIERN OU LES MALHEURS DU LIBERTINAGE, *drame en trois actes et en prose, par D.-A.-F.-S. Représenté au théâtre Molière, à Paris en 1791 et à Versailles. . . . l'an VIII de la République. A Versailles, chez Blaisot, libraire, rue Satory, an VIII* [1800]. 8vo.

9. LES CRIMES DE L'AMOUR OU LE DÉLIRE DES PASSIONS. *Nouvelles historiques et tragiques, précédées d'une Idée sur les romans et ornées de gravures, par D. A. F. Sade, auteur d'Aline et Valcour. A Paris, chez Massé, Editeur-propiétaire, rue Helvétius, No. 580. an VIII* [1800]. 4 volumes, 12mo. Four frontispieces. The contents are:

Vol. I,   *Juliette et Raunai ou la Conspiration d'Amboise; La Double Epreuve.*

Vol. II,   *Miss Henriette Stralson ou les Effets de désespoir; Faxelange ou les torts de l'ambition; Florville et Courval ou le Fatalisme.*

Vol. III,   *Rodrigue ou la Tour enchantée; Laurence et Antonio; Ernestine.*

Vol. IV,   *Dorgeville ou le Criminal par Vertu; La Comtesse de Sancerre ou la Rivale de sa fille; Eugénie de Franval*

10. ZOLOÉ ET SES DEUX ACOLYTES, OU QUELQUES DÉCADES DE LA VIE DE TROIS JOLIES FEMMES; *Histoire véritable du siècle dernier: Par un contemporain. A Turin; se trouve à Paris, chez tous les marchands de nouveautés. De l'Imprimerie de l'auteur, Messidor, an VIII* [1800]. 12mo. Frontispiece representing Mmes. Tallien, Visconti, and Joséphine de Beauharnais.

11. L'AUTEUR DES CRIMES DE L'AMOUR A VILLETERQUE, FOLLICULAIRE, *Paris, Massé, an IX* [1801]. 12mo. 19pp.

POLITICAL PAMPHLETS

1. ADDRESSE D'UN CITOYEN DE PARIS AU ROI DES FRANÇAIS. Paris, no date. 8vo.
2. IDÉE SUR LE MODE DE LA SANCTION DES LOIX. Paris, no date [1792]. 8vo.
3. PROJET DE PÉTITION DES SECTIONS DE PARIS A LA CONVENTION NATIONALE. Paris, no date. 8vo.
4. DISCOURS PRONONCÉ A LA FÊTE DÉCERNÉE PAR LA SECTION DES PIQUES, AUX MANES DE MARAT ET DE LA PELLETIER. *Par Sade, citoyen de cette section et membre de la Société populaire de la Section des Piques.* Paris, no date [1793]. 8vo.
5. PETITION DE LA SECTION DES PIQUES AUX REPRÉSENTANS DU PEUPLE FRANCAIS. Paris, 1793. 8vo.

1. DORCI OU LA BIZARRERIE DU SORT. *Conte inédit per le Marquis de Sade, publié sur le manuscrit avec une notice sur l'auteur* (Signed A.F., Anatole France). Paris, 1881.12mo.

2. LES 120 JOURNÉES DE SODOME OU L'ÉCOLE DE LIBERTINAGE, *Par le Marquis de Sade. Publié pour la première fois d'après le manuscrit original, avec des annotations scientifiques, par le Docteur Eugen Dühren.* Paris, Club des Bibliophiles, 1904. 4to.

3. LES 120 JOURNÉES DE SODOME, OU L'ÉCOLE DE LIBERTINAGE, *par le Marquis de Sade. Edition critique, établie sur le manuscrit original autographe par Maurice Heine.* Paris, S. et C., by subscription. 3 volumes, 4to, 1931-1935.

4. HISTORIETTES, CONTES ET FABLIAUX *de Donatien-Alphonse-François Marquis de Sade, publiés pour la première fois sur les manuscrits autographe inédits par Maurice Heine.* Paris, for the Société du Roman Philosophique, 1926. 2 volumes, 4to.
   Contains: *Le Serpent; L'heureuse feinte; le M— puni; l'Evêque embourbé; le Revenant; Les Harangueurs provençaux; Attrapezmol toujours de même; L'Epoux complaisant; Aventure incompréhensible; La Fleur de Châtaignier; L'Instituteur philosophe; La Prude ou la Recontre Imprévue; Emile de Tourville ou la Cruauté fraternelle; Augustine de Villeblanche, ou le Stratagème de l'Amour; Soit fait ainsi qu'il est requis; Le Président mystifié; La Marquis de Télème ou les Effets du Libertinage; Le Talion; Le Cocu de lui-même ou le Raccommodement imprévu; Il y a place pour deux; L'Epoux corrigé; Le Mari prêtre, conte provençal; La Châtelaine de Longeville ou la Femme vengée; Les Filous.*

5. DIALOGUE ENTRE UN PRÊTE ET UN MORRIBOND *par 'Donatien Alphonse- François Marquis de Sade, publié pour la première fois . . . avec une avant-propos et notes par Maurice Heine.* Paris, Stendhal et Cie, 1926. 4to.

6. LES INFORTUNES DE LA VERTU. *Texte établi sur le manuscrit original autographe et publié pour la premiere fois avec une introduction par Maurice Heine.* Paris, 1930. 8vo. The first version of *Justine.*

II

WORKS ATTRIBUTED TO SADE

1. PAULINE ET BELVAL OU VICTIMES DE L'AMOUR CRIMINEL, *ancedote parisienne du XVIIe sièce.* Paris, [1798]. 3 volumes, 12mo. With engravings.

1a. PAULINE ET BELVAL, ON SUITES FUNESTES D'UN AMOUR CRIMINEL, *ancedote récente. Par M. R. —.* Paris, 1812. 2 volumes, 12mo. Frontispiece.

2. LA MARQUISE DE GANGES. Paris, Béchet, 1813. 2 volumes, 8vo.

3. LA FRANCE FOUTUE, *tragédie lubrique et royaliste*, in 3 acts and verse. A BARBE-EN-CON, *en Foutro-manie, l'an des fouteurs*, 1796. 18mo.

4. VALMOR ET LYDIA, *ou Voyage autour du monde de deux amants qui se cherchaint.* Paris [1799]. 3 volumes in 1, 12mo.

5. ALZONDE ET KORADIN. Paris, 1799. 2 volumes, 12mo.

III

UNPUBLISHED MANUSCRIPTS

PLAYS

1. L'ÉCOLE DES JALOUX, OU LA FOLLE EPREUVE. A one-act play in vers libre.

2. FRANCHISE ET TRAHISON. A prose drama in three acts.

3. LE MISANTHROPE PAR AMOUR, OU SOPHIE ET DESFRANCS. A five-act play in vers libre, with entr'actes.

4. LE CAPRICIEUX, OU L'HOMME INÉGAL. A verse play in five acts.

5. LA FÊTE DE L'AMITIÉ, *encadrant un prologue et un vaudeville ayant pour titre: Hommage à la reconnaissance.* In two acts, incorporating prose, verse, and vaudeville.

6. LA TOUR MYSTÉRIEUSE, A one-act *opéra-comique.*

7. *Azélis, ou la Coquette punie.* A pantomime in one act, in vers libre.

8. LES JUMELLES, OU LE CHOIX DIFFICILE. A two-act play in verse.

9. LE PRÉVARICATEUR, OU LE MAGISTRAT DU TEMPS PASSÉ. A play in five acts in verse.

10. HENRIETTE DE SAINT-CLAIR, OU LA FORCE DU SANG. A five-act prose drama.

11. JEANNE LAISNÉ, OU LE SIEGE DE BEAUVAIS. A five-act tragedy in verse.

12. FANNI, OU LES EFFETS DU DÉSESPOIR. A three-act prose drama.

13. L'UNION DES ARTS, OU LES RUSES DE L'AMOUR. A play in alexandrines, in vers libre, prose, music, and vaudeville.

14. LES ANTIQUARES. A play in one act, in prose.

15. L'ÉGAREMENT DE L'INFORTUNE. In three acts.

16. LE PÉRE DE FAMILLE. In three acts.

17. TANCRÉDE. In one act, with verse and music.

18. CLÉOTINE, OU LA FILLE MALHEUREUSE. In three acts.

20. LE BOUDOIR.

21. LA DOUBLE INTRIGUE.

22. JULIA, OU LE MARIAGE SANS FEMME. A *folie-vaudeville* in one act.

NOVELS

1. ADÉLAIDE DE BRUNSWICK, *princesse de Saxe, événement du XIe siècle.*
2. HISTOIRE SECRÈTE D'ISABELLE DE BAVIÈRE, *reine de France, dans la guelle se trouvent des faits rares et inconnus, ou restés dans l'oubli jusqu'à ce jour et soigneusement étayés de manuscrits authentiques, allemands, anglais et latins.* To be published, Paris Gallimard, 1953.
3. CONRAD. Dealing with the Albigenses; it was seized by the authorities in 1803 when Sade was transferred to Charenton.
4. MARCEL.
5. PHOLOÉ ET ZÉNOCRATE. In epistolary form, and unfinished. ..
6. LES JOURNÉES DE FLORABELLE. . . . Cf. Chronology, entry for April 25, 1807.

MISCELLANEOUS

1. LE PORTEFEUILLE D'UN HOMME DE LETTRES. 4 volumes.
2. 11 manuscript books, a journal of Sade's imprisonment at Vincennes and in the Bastille, 1770-1789. Partly written in cipher. Said to have been destroyed.
3. MÉMOIRES. An outline, with fragments.
4. UN PLAN DE MAISON PUBLIQUE.
5. PROJET D'UN COMBAT DE GLADIATEURS.
6. CONTES, *etc., par le marquis de Sade.* 20 notebooks bound together, dated 1785. 494 pp. In the Bibliothéque Nationale, and partly published by Maurice Heine in *Historiettes*, etc., 1926, *q.v.*

* * *

Apart from these, since 1833 various fragments, letters, notes, etc., have been published in journals and periodicals.

NEL BESTSELLERS

Crime

W002 773	THE LIGHT OF DAY	*Eric Ambler*	25p
W002 786	ABILITY TO KILL	*Eric Ambler*	25p
W002 799	THE MURDER LEAGUE	*Robert L. Fish*	30p
W002 876	MURDER MUST ADVERTISE	*Dorothy L. Sayers*	35p
W002 849	STRONG POISON	*Dorothy L. Sayers*	30p
W002 848	CLOUDS OF WITNESS	*Dorothy L. Sayers*	35p
W002 845	THE DOCUMENTS IN THE CASE	*Dorothy L. Sayers*	30p
W002 877	WHOSE BODY*	*Dorothy L. Sayers*	30p
W002 749	THE NINE TAILORS	*Dorothy L. Sayers*	30p
W002 871	THE UNPLEASANTNESS AT THE BELLONA CLUB		
		Dorothy L. Sayers	30p
W002 750	FIVE RED HERRINGS	*Dorothy L. Sayers*	30p
W002 826	UNNATURAL DEATH	*Dorothy L. Sayers*	30p
W003 011	GAUDY NIGHT	*Dorothy L. Sayers*	40p
W002 870	BLOODY MAMA	*Robert Thom*	25p

Fiction

W002 755	PAID SERVANT	*E. R. Braithwaite*	30p
T005 801	RIFIFI IN NEW YORK	*Auguste le Breton*	30p
W002 833	THE CRAZY LADIES	*Joyce Elbert*	40p
W002 743	HARRISON HIGH	*John Farris*	40p
W002 861	THE GIRL FROM HARRISON HIGH	*John Farris*	40p
T007 030	A TIME OF PREDATORS	*Joe Gores*	30p
W002 424	CHILDREN OF KAYWANA	*Edgar Mittelholzer*	37½p
W002 425	KAYWANA STOCK	*Edgar Mittelholzer*	37½p
W002 426	KAYWANA BLOOD	*Edgar Mittelholzer*	37½p
T009 084	SIR, YOU BASTARD	*G. F. Newman*	30p
W002 881	THE FORTUNATE PILGRIM	*Mario Puzo*	35p
W002 752	THE HARRAD EXPERIMENT	*Robert H. Rimmer*	30p
W002 920	PROPOSITION 31	*Robert H. Rimmer*	30p
W002 427	THE ZOLOTOV AFFAIR	*Robert H. Rimmer*	25p
W002 704	THE REBELLION OF YALE MARRATT	*Robert H. Rimmer*	30p
W002 896	THE CARPETBAGGERS	*Harold Robbins*	75p
W002 918	THE ADVENTURERS	*Harold Robbins*	75p
W002 941	A STONE FOR DANNY FISHER	*Harold Robbins*	50p
W002 654	NEVER LOVE A STRANGER	*Harold Robbins*	60p
W002 653	THE DREAM MERCHANTS	*Harold Robbins*	60p
W002 917	WHERE LOVE HAS GONE	*Harold Robbins*	60p
W002 155	NEVER LEAVE ME	*Harold Robbins*	25p
T006 743	THE INHERITORS	*Harold Robbins*	60p
T009 467	STILETTO	*Harold Robbins*	30p
W002 761	THE SEVEN MINUTES	*Irving Wallace*	75p
W002 580	THE BEAUTIFUL COUPLE	*William Woolfolk*	37½p
W002 312	BRIDE OF LIBERTY	*Frank Yerby*	25p
W002 479	AN ODOUR OF SANCTITY	*Frank Yerby*	50p
W002 916	BENTON'S ROW	*Frank Yerby*	40p
W002 822	GILLIAN	*Frank Yerby*	40p
W002 895	CAPTAIN REBEL	*Frank Yerby*	30p
W003 010	THE VIXENS	*Frank Yerby*	40p
W003 007	A WOMAN CALLED FANCY	*Frank Yerby*	30p

Science Fiction

T009 696	GLORY ROAD	*Robert Heinlein*	40p
W002 844	STRANGER IN A STRANGE LAND	*Robert Heinlein*	60p
W002 386	PODKAYNE OF MARS	*Robert Heinlein*	30p
W002 449	THE MOON IS A HARSH MISTRESS	*Robert Heinlein*	40p
W002 630	THE MAN WHO SOLD THE MOON	*Robert Heinlein*	30p
W002 754	DUNE	*Frank Herbert*	60p
W002 911	SANTAROGA BARRIER	*Frank Herbert*	30p
W002 641	NIGHT WALK	*Bob Shaw*	25p
W002 716	SHADOW OF HEAVEN	*Bob Shaw*	25p

War

Western

Walt Slade—Bestsellers

General

Mad

- - - - - - - - - - - -

EL P.O. BOX 11 FALMOUTH CORNWALL

Please send cheque or postal order. Allow 5p per book to cover tage and packing (Overseas 6p per book).

e ....

ss ....

....

....